The Age of Ages

and the

Christian's Future

The Hope Beyond Heaven

LEE R. BRUNER

ISBN 978-1-64670-642-6 (Paperback)
ISBN 978-1-64670-643-3 (Hardcover)
ISBN 978-1-64670-644-0 (Digital)

Covenant Books, Inc.
11661 Hwy 707
Murrells Inlet, SC 29576
www.covenantbooks.com

Contents

PREFACE

This book is primarily for the Christian, but anyone who reads its pages will be enriched by its content. All should understand the full and complete gospel of the Lord Jesus Christ. The Christians' hope, when fully understood, is the greatest promise ever given to any being in all of God's creation. When the good news is revealed, it gives the believer what I call "hold-on power." Hold-on power is what the Christian receives when the Holy Spirit makes known in his or her being that everything in the gospel is true and, therefore, worthy of holding on to. The truths written in this book do just that—and also for all non-Christian readers. You will find a Christian perspective on aliens, UFOs, and whether there is life on other planets. Was there life on earth before the emergence of man? Where do demons come from, and did God make them? What is the future for all of creation? These and many, many more questions will be addressed by this revelation; but most importantly, the reader will learn what happens in the universe when all who are going to heaven are admitted, and the kingdom of God is instituted. It is my hope that all who read will understand the full scope of the unsearchable riches of Christ and, just like me, repent and receive the Lord Jesus Christ and this wonderful hope.

INTRODUCTION

Eyes have not seen, nor ear heard, neither have entered into the heart of man, the things which God hath prepared for them that love Him. But God hath revealed them unto us by His Spirit; for the Spirit searcheth all things, yea the deep things of God.

—1 Corinthians 2:9–10

The Christian's hope is the greatest encouragement ever promised by God. It should be fully comprehended and sought out by every believer so it can provide the strength God intended for it to give to us. The more we know, the greater our faith and joy in that hope in which we believe. God has amazing plans for the Christian—a future that is so glorious, the Bible says, "Eyes have not seen, nor ear have heard." This does not mean that it is hidden until the believer goes to heaven, for God's Word states, "God hath revealed them unto us by His Spirit." This book is a focus on the deep things of God as they are revealed by His Spirit through His Word. It is a revelation of what will happen to the Christian after he goes to heaven. The Greek word for revelation is *apokalupis*, and it means to unveil, reveal, and uncover; or the lifting up of a curtain so that all may see alike what was previously veiled. The revelation of God is the unveiling of facts and truths, which man himself could not know but are divinely revealed by the Spirit of God. My prayer is that all may see the wondrous grace and goodness of God toward those who believe and that those who do believe receive Holy Spirit enablement to apprehend this truth and have it communicated to their spirit, for it is by the Spirit that we know. I want the reader of this revelation to understand the most important part of my interpretation of scripture. That is which that exalts God and magnifies Him and His work is the correct revelation and that which lessens or contradicts Him is error. So, what is an *age*?

The Greek word for "age" is *aion*, and it means a period of time, whether long or short. In this sense, there are many ages: creative, past, present, and future ages to come. In order to explain the wonderful plan of God, let us go back to the beginning.

CHAPTER 1

The Creative Age

This age in the dateless past includes the time God created the universe and all things therein. "In the beginning God created the heaven and the earth" (Genesis 1:1). Here, in the time when God first made the universe, it is of utmost importance to understand how He made it. The Hebrew word *bara* is translated "created" and means to bring into being or existence for the first time. Genesis 1:1 in the amplified translation reads this way: "In the beginning God (Elohim) created (by forming from nothing) the heavens and the earth." Verse 1 marks the beginning of all things, when everything was first made in this time in the dateless past. Was the earth and the universe quiet? Was the earth created uninhabited? Is the Bible silent about this age? First, the question must be asked, "How does God create? Did He first *bara* the earth and the universe to be without form and void, lifeless spheres in a vast space that have no real purpose?" Know this, God is perfect in all His ways, and it is not logical or accurate to suggest that He made anything less than perfect. Isaiah 45:18 (Amplified) gives us insight into how God creates: "For the Lord, who created the heavens (He is God who formed the earth and made it; He established it and *did not create it to be a wasteland, but formed it to be inhabited*) says this, I am the Lord, and there is no one else." Notice that when God first created (*bara*) the earth, it was not an uninhabited wasteland. God is not incomplete or unfinished in His pursuits. He is the Great Architect and Master Builder of all things. "As for God, His way is perfect," Psalm 18:30 proclaims, and Deuteronomy 32:4 confirms the manner in which God creates: "He is the rock, His work is *perfect*; for all his ways are judgment: A God of truth and without iniquity; just and right is He." The word *perfect* in these verses is translated from the Hebrew word *tamiym*, which means blameless and without blemish or spot, *complete* in the sense of the entire or whole thing. So we see that if God creates, He does it perfectly and completely without flaw or shortcoming. If He says He made it not to be a wasteland, then it wasn't. If He says He made it to be inhabited, then it was. He completes His work! When we read in Genesis 1:2, "And the earth was without form, and void; and darkness was upon the face of the deep," we must understand that this is describing the earth after it had already been first made. Something happened to it. Something changed it from the way God created it initially. The Hebrew word for form is *tohuw*, and means "to lie waste, a desolation, a worthless or vain thing." *Void* in the Hebrew is *bohuw* and means "to be empty." *Was* in verse 2 is from the Hebrew word *haya*, which means "became." To read Genesis 1:2 in the original Hebrew language, *haya-tohuw va bohuw*, it would read like this: "and the earth became desolate and empty." It contradicts God's perfection and His Word to believe that He made the earth and the universe this way. When we see "and the spirit of God moved upon the face of the waters," we are viewing the reconstruction of what had become a fallen earth. God comes down and restores earth to a second habitable state. He is not creating it for the first time, the time when it was so glorious that all the angels shouted for joy (Job 38:4–7). Verse 1 is a description of this time, and verse 2 is describing God's reconstruction. It *became* a wasteland and uninhabited but was not created that way at first. Verse 2 introduces the history of humanity and all the animals made on earth and in the seas. Man can trace time to this beginning somewhere around five or six thousand years, but the earth is much, much older—millions and possibly billions of years older. We call this the dateless past because there is no way of knowing when God first created it. Even though we don't know when He created it, the Bible is not silent about what was happening in the universe and on earth in the time when they were first created. We know the worlds were not wastelands, nor were they unin-habited. Consider what God told Adam and Eve in Genesis 1:28: "Be fruitful and multiply, and *replenish* the earth." God told them to *make full and complete again* by multiplying their offspring upon the earth. God's Word tells us that there was a civilization of inhabitants on the earth before Adam. You can't *replenish* something that has not been *plenished* before. We know that they perished and that they were not exactly like Adam because Adam was made in the direct image of God Himself and therefore very important, so important, in fact, that God became man so that He could redeem man back to Himself. That world that then was, being overflowed with water perished and did not receive the grace and forgiveness of God. These unfortunate earthlings, whom Adam and Eve replaced on the earth, perished without mercy. To understand the fate of that social system, we must go back to the dateless past, to that dispensation in time when they lived, back to the time when angels ruled the universe on behalf of God.

CHAPTER 2

The Dispensation of Angels

What is a dispensation? The word "dispensation" comes from two Greek words: *oikos*, which means a house or stewardship, and *nomos*, which means a law. Together *oiko-nomos* means a *stewardship of law*. As applied to various ages, it means a moral or probationary period in human and angelic history in which God tests free moral agents according to a fixed standard of conduct or responsibility, under which they are to remain true to God and rule for Him on the earth or elsewhere in the universe. All occupants of God's worlds must abide by His stewardship of law. This is clearly seen in Genesis 2:15–17,

> And the Lord God took the man and put Him
> into the Garden of Eden to dress it and to keep it
> and the Lord God commanded the man, saying,
> of every tree of the garden thou mayest freely eat,
> but of the tree of the knowledge of good and evil,
> thou shalt not eat of it; for in the day that thou
> eatest thereof thou shalt surely die.

See the standard of conduct not to touch the tree of knowledge of good and evil and what the penalty would be if he violated it? So the social system that *existed*—that Adam and Eve replaced—no doubt broke God's law. The Bible gives great light on this probationary period in the dateless past when angels ruled the planets for God. *Moses*, as we have seen in Genesis, taught that the earth had inhabitants before God made Adam and Eve and articulated that the earth *became* desolate and empty. *Isaiah* taught that the angel Lucifer ruled the earth before Adam and that he fell to the earth after leading a rebellion into heaven to overthrow *God*. Isaiah 14:12–15 recalls,

> How art thou fallen from heaven, o Lucifer, son of the morning! How art thou cut down to the ground, which didst weaken the nations! For thou hast said in thine heart, I will *ascend* into heaven, I will exalt *my throne* above the stars of God; I will sit also upon the mount of the congregation, in the sides of the north; I will *ascend* above the heights of the clouds: I will be like the Most High. Yet thou shalt be brought down to hell, to the sides of the pit.

Here we see what happened on earth when Lucifer ruled earth for God in the age called the dispensation of angels. First, we see him weakening the nations, but which nations? It certainly wasn't any modern nations because the time of this event took place in the dateless past, millions of years before God even made Adam. Nations in Hebrew is translated *gentiles* and *heathen* and is never translated angels. Lucifer weakened the people that he ruled on earth. Again, these nations of earthlings were not like Adam, for he is made in the direct image of God and created with the specific purpose of replacing fallen angels. Upon deceiving the nations, Lucifer convinces a third of the angels who ruled on their own worlds to rebel with him. Please note that astronomers say there are about forty sextillion stars, which are suns to other planets like our sun in our solar system. One tenth of the planets is in a temperate zone that could sustain life, they tell us. We know God made them to be inhabited and fruitful because that's the way He creates. When we see in Revelation 12:7–9 the war in heaven between God's angels led by Michael against Satan and his angels, we must ask the question,

"When did they become Satan's angels?" They became his subjects when they yielded to his rebellious plan of overthrowing the rule of God and taking the planets for themselves. Consider the rule of scripture concerning servanthood: "Know ye not, that to whom ye yield yourselves servants to obey, His servants ye are to whom ye obey" (Romans 6:16). Revelation 12:4 describes a third part of the stars of heaven who were deceived into following the dragon, that old serpent called the devil and Satan. Angels are called stars because they are the illuminated ones whose authority lights their planets. They received light from God and communicated it to their worlds. Lucifer is called Son of the Morning for this very reason. Isaiah 14:12 in the Amplified translation reads this way: "How you have fallen from heaven, O *star* of the morning (light bringer)." God communicated His light to the worlds through His delegated authorities, His holy angles. One can only imagine the wonder of the worlds that were united under the eternal wisdom and splendor of the Great "Elohim." Satan said in his heart, "I will ascend into heaven, I will exalt my throne above the stars of God." Now in order to ascend to heaven, he must be beneath it, and in order to exalt his throne, he must have one from which he rules. He, looking up from earth, seeking to exalt himself, looked past the other planets into the third heaven where God's throne is, and he proclaims, "I will preside on the mountain of the gods far away in the north" (verse 13, NLT). In verse 14, notice that he has to ascend past the clouds, which proves his throne was on the earth under the clouds. It is obvious Lucifer was not ruling some part of heaven, for he ascended with a third of the angels into heaven and was cast down. Jesus Himself spoke of this event in the dateless past in Luke 10:18: "And He (Jesus) said unto them, I beheld Satan as lightning fall from heaven." Ezekiel taught the fall of Lucifer and the overthrow of the pre-Adamite world. Look at Ezekiel 28:12–19. Verse 12 states that "he sealest up the sum," which means he is the perfect pattern for all of creation. He is perfect in beauty and full of wisdom. One cannot comprehend the technologies and advancements of the world under such government. His throne was in Eden, the garden of God. This Eden was the one on the original earth before God made Adam. It was the garden God made for Lucifer to rule from. (God later prepared a garden for Adam to rule from on the renovated earth.)

Verse 13 also describes the state of the garden of God under Lucifer: "Every precious stone was thy covering." Imagine a world rich and fruitful with no curse or deficiency. The earth before Lucifer's rebellion was a stunning masterpiece. This beautiful and enlightened age when earth was first made featured mountains of diamonds and valleys of sapphire. We cannot overstate how glorious the earth was, nor can we the wisdom and engineering marvels that these earthlings enjoyed. Lucifer's amazing wisdom and anointing gave him astounding insights to govern the society. Wisdom in Hebrew is *chokmah* and refers to technical skills or special abilities in fashioning something. The same word is found in Exodus 35:31, where it also denotes special ability to build and produce workmanship. We cannot know how this society lived, but we know that it exceeded and surpassed ours in every way. Ezekiel shows us three distinct characteristics of dispensations: civilization, community, and government. Lucifer's rebellion caused his government to sin against the civilizations he was anointed to *cover*. Instead of leading the communities on earth into worship and subjugation to the Elohim, he went from city to city and to the great *sanctuaries* of every community, where all were to be led into worship and receive the governance of God. Instead, he began to slander and stir the inhabitants of earth into open rebellion.

> Thou hast defiled thy sanctuaries by the multitude of thine iniquities, by the iniquity of thy traffic; therefore, will I bring forth a fire from the midst of thee, it shall devour thee, and I will bring thee to ashes *upon the earth* in the sight of all them that behold thee. (verse 18)

Notice that the nations that Lucifer weakened beheld him when God cast him down to the earth. Lucifer, through his great beauty, wisdom, and ability, had convinced a third of the angels and his own subjects on earth to rebel! Now the terrifying reality of their insurrection is realized. Their leader and commander in chief has been cast down from heaven. Verse 19 in the Amplified translation says, "All the peoples (nations) who *knew you* are appalled at you; you have come to a horrible and terrifying end and will forever cease to be." What about these earthlings who fell under the authority of Lucifer? They are not angels but are an intelligent humanoid civilization who willingly followed Lucifer. Now the once-sinless world had become sinful, and all who were once in unity with God had now become his adversaries. Satan is the new name of Lucifer, for he is now the adversary of God. God will not allow him to remain the ruler of His planet and immediately launches a counteroffensive upon Satan and his forces. The fallen angels and all the inhabitants of their worlds make up the rebellious army of the devil. Ephesians 6:11–12 in the New Living translation says,

> Put on all of God's armor so that you will be able to stand firm against all strategies of the devil. For we are not fighting against flesh and blood enemies, but against evil rulers and authorities of the unseen world, against mighty powers in this dark world, and against evil spirits in the heavenly places.

It is a fact that Satan had an army, and they are cursed to follow him forever because of the choice they made to follow him and rebel with him in the dateless past. I suppose you could call what happens next "Star Wars or the invasion of earth" because God comes down from heaven and overthrows all the cities and authorities of those that rebelled with Satan. Jeremiah gives us details of this time when God puts down this rebellion and destroys these worlds and their civilizations. Jeremiah 4:23–26 states,

> I beheld the earth, and, lo, it was without form, and void; and the heavens, and they had no light. I beheld the mountains, and, lo, they trembled, and all the hills moved lightly. I beheld, and, lo, there was no man, and all the birds of the heav-

ens were fled. I beheld, and, lo, the fruitful place
was a wilderness, and all the cities thereof were
broken down at the presence of the Lord, and by
his fierce anger.

Jeremiah, like Moses, had insight into the earth becoming *tohuw
va bohuw* but gives us a much fuller revelation to how. He pictures an
angry God coming to execute justice on Satan and the pre-Adamite
world that he led into rebellion. Notice the heavens are also mentioned in this judgment because those ruling angels suffered the same
fate as their leader. What we see happening to earth also happened to
the worlds that they ruled. All cities were destroyed. All vegetation,
men (humanoid), and animals were totally destroyed. The fact that
there never will be times in the future from our day or through all
eternity when the earth will be totally desolate proves emphatically
that these events happened long before Adam. God invades and pronounces judgment. He defeats the angels who flee from Him and
destroys everything in a mighty flood. All the humanoids in the earth
are totally overwhelmed by the wrath of the waters, and they perish!
"And darkness was upon the face of the deep" (Genesis 1:2) illumi-
nates in the dispensation of angels in the dateless past, God destroyed
that world that then was with a mighty flood. That's why you see "the
Spirit of God moving upon the face of the waters." He didn't create
it this way, but as a result of Lucifer's fall and the judgment of God,
it became this way. Know this: when God first creates, He does it
perfect. It is true that God made everything, angels and humanoid
alike. However, He is not responsible for what His free moral agents
do after He gives them life. "Thou wast perfect in thy ways from the
day that thou wast created, till iniquity was found in thee." Yes, God
created Lucifer, but he decided to become the devil. Yes, God created
the earthlings that Lucifer ruled on earth, but their decision to rebel
caused them to become disembodied spirits known to us in the Bible
as evil spirits. God does not create evil spirits. He only creates perfect and good, but like their master, they became devils. The word
"demon" is not mentioned in the Bible, but it simply means a devil.
These humanoids died in the destruction of Satan's world, and now

their disembodied spirits are forever under the control of the devil. There were males and females in Lucifer's civilization and, therefore, *male and female* devils. Peter the apostle taught that there was a social world that was totally destroyed by a great flood: "Whereby *the world that then was*, being overflowed with water, perished" (2 Peter 3:6). The word "world" in the Greek translation is *kosmos* and means a social system. The word "perished" is *aapollumi* in Greek and means to destroy fully and completely. In this particular flood, everything was completely destroyed: people, animals, vegetation—everything. This cannot refer to Noah's flood because the flood of Noah did not destroy all the social system on earth between Adam to Noah. Noah and his family and all the animals continued the social system that began with Adam and Eve, and it continues to this day. In fact, Peter is referring to two distinct worlds and describes the manner in which both will be and was destroyed. The world that then was perished by water. "But the heavens and the earth, *which are now*, by the same word are kept in store, reserved unto fire against the day of judgment and perdition of ungodly men" (2 Peter 3:7). The second social system will perish by a purging fire. This present sinful Adamite social system will come to an end! The two statements—"*the world that then was*" and "the heavens and earth *which are now*"—prove two separate social systems on earth. One was before the one which is now. Satan's rule on earth ended, and all his angels' rule in the heavens ended as well. Having seen that God uses His faithful subjects to rule planets on His behalf and for His glory, let us remember that some—not all—of the angels fell with Lucifer. Since our solar system is about six billion miles across, and our galaxy, called the Milky Way, contains about two billion stars, which are suns each with its own family of planets, would it be improper to suggest that those angels who did not fail God are still ruling on his behalf? The Bible teaches that the heavens are inhabited.

> For through him (Jesus) God created everything in the *heavenly realms* and on earth, He made the things we can see and the things we can't see, such as thrones, kingdoms, rulers, and authorities *in*

the unseen world. Everything was created through
Him and for Him. (Colossians 1:16)

This reveals that there are thrones and civilizations in the heavens, and it is one of the most remarkable facts of scripture, and they are created by Him and for Him. One important purpose of the worlds is for them to be inhabited and pronounce glory and praise to the Creator. The universe is vast beyond conception and no wonder because it is hard to conceive that a God existing from all eternity was not doing anything until He finally decided to make the earth. The fact of the matter is God has been making things in all eternity past. Jeremiah 33:22 says, "As the host of heaven cannot be numbered, neither the sand of the sea measured." The host of heaven cannot be counted! Psalm 104:2 says, "God stretches out the heavens like a curtain," and Isaiah 48:13 states, "My right hand hath spanned the heavens; when I call unto them, they stand together." Yes, there is life on distant planets, and they are being governed by God's faithful subjects. Our fallen universe will be restored, and its worlds will be inhabited again.

CHAPTER 3

The Importance of Adam

Now, after the rebellion of Lucifer and the fall of a third of the worlds, God must now move to bring His vast kingdom back into unity and order under Him. All of creation is watching. This part of His kingdom is dark and lifeless because of the war with its inhabitants. Satan and His forces are out there hiding in terror, wondering what happens next. The mighty Elohim enacts the plan. God's worlds must be inhabited and governed by faithful subjects. All things must exalt God! They return to the place where the rebellion and insurrection started. They (Elohim) return to earth. The start of all life in the universe must start here because this is where all life in the universe ended. The plan of God was to renovate the worlds He destroyed in the war with Satan and his angels and replace them with a special new creation. The starting place must be earth! People have often asked me, "Why does Satan hate mankind so much?" Here is the answer: because we were all created specifically to take His place! Satan once governed earth. He is bound to it even though he is removed as its ruler. One day, he knows he will be locked in the special prison prepared for him and all that rebelled with him. Jesus said, "Depart from me, ye cursed, into everlasting fire, prepared for the devil and his angels" (Matthew 25:41).

His prison was made in the center of the earth, and he has no choice; he cannot escape his fate. Hell was not made for the sons of Adam, so no human has to go there. But if one serves Satan and follows his rebellious way against God, He will go the way of his master. "Yet thou shalt be brought down to hell to the sides of the pit," Isaiah 14:15 declares concerning Satan. God starts over. This time, He will create a different being, like the holy angels in power and light but also like the humanoid nations with their ability to procreate. He will, after all, have the mission of replenishing the worlds. Consider Genesis 1:26–28, where we see just how special God makes Adam. Verse 26: "And God said, Let *us* make man in our *image*, after our *likeness*. And let them have dominion over the fish of the sea, and over the fowl of the air, and over the cattle, and over every creeping thing that creepeth upon the earth." First of all, all of creation is awestruck because the mighty Elohim is about to make something in His *image* and *likeness*. The Hebrew word for "image" is *tselem* and means "shade, resemblance of the outward form." *Likeness* is *demuwth* in Hebrew and means "resemblance and shape." So Adam's color and the shape of his body resembles God. Genesis 2:7 states, "And the Lord God formed man of the dust of the ground, and breathed into his nostrils the breath of life: and man became a living soul." Man's body was formed from the mud of the earth, but his spirit and soul were created when God breathed His own breath into him. Adam is now alive, and what a life it is! He looks like the Elohim. *Elohim* is Hebrew for "Gods." It is a uniplural noun and refers to the Godhead. Hence, "Let *us* make man in *our* image after *our* likeness." So not only does Adam look like the gods, but he is animated and created by a very personal part from Him. His breath—the immortal, all-powerful breath of God—into the body, created an immortal soul. Man was created to never die. He will have the task of populating the worlds, and that's going to take quite some time. We see that God puts Himself in man, for he is to be the light for the worlds. He is to be its covering and provider because he is like his Creator and given incredible ability. He is given dominion over the earth and everything in it. Since the Bible is primarily concerned with the earth, it is not always easy to see God's plan for man in the heavens; but again, the scriptures are not silent. Adam was given dominion over the heavens. Consider Psalm 8:3–6.

> When I consider thy heavens, the work of thy fingers, the moon and the stars, which thou hast ordained; what is man that thou art mindful of him? And the son of man, that thou visitest him? For thou hast made him a little lower than the angels, and hast *crowned him* with glory and honour. *Thou madest him to have dominion over the works of thy hands*; thou hast put *all things* under his feet.

Adam is made *the god* of this world and given the dominion over everything, moon and stars included. When I say god, you must understand this is the term God uses for his magistrates or rulers who have great authority. Consider the words of Jesus to the Jews in John 10:34–35: "It is written in your own scriptures that God said to certain leaders of the people, I say, *you are gods!* And you know that the Scriptures cannot be altered. So, if those *people* who received God's message were *called gods*." In the very beginning of Adam's rule, he was given great authority. In fact, what he said mattered, and God gave him credence over everything. In Genesis 2:19, we see God deferring to Adam on what every living creature that He made would be called.

> And out of the ground the Lord God formed every beast of the field, and every fowl of the air, and brought them unto Adam to see what he would call them;
> And whatsoever Adam called *every* living creature, that was the name thereof!

We must mention the incredible light and ability in which Adam walked. He had God-breathed intellect and powers. I don't believe anyone today could call a bear an elephant or a horse an eagle.

It just wouldn't work. I also believe that since he is made like God that he had more ability and gifting than the first ruler of the earth, Lucifer, himself. He is more than a suitable replacement for him in governing the earth. "And the Lord God planted a garden eastward in Eden: and there He put the man whom He had formed" (Genesis 2:8). Just like Lucifer's throne was in Eden, God now renovates this paradise for Adam to rule from. He is to start here in Eden on the earth and repopulate the worlds. It is a glorious time in all of God's kingdom. The plan of God to restore all fallen universes back into right standing with Him is received with great joy.

CHAPTER 4

Satan's Intervention

S omeone else is viewing this move of God upon the earth with great dismay and agony. Lucifer once ruled this majestic sphere, and now out of fellowship with his Creator is become Satan, the adversary. He is not happy with the creation of man because it begins the judgment of him and his followers. It won't be long before he will be imprisoned forever in the very world that he once ruled. He must dwarf the plan of God. He must find a way to delay the inevitable. He's there in the garden, lurking like a lion seeking its prey. He's watching and probing for weaknesses in man. "How can I reclaim my earth," he asks? Adam is too powerful to attack head on. He is in perfect unity with God and has complete authority over everything. In fact, God told Adam to be on the lookout for Satan and his evil powers. In Genesis 2:15—"And the Lord God took the man and put him into the Garden of Eden to dress it and to keep it"—Adam is given the task to *keep* the garden. *Keep* in the Hebrew translation is *shamar* and means to hedge about, guard, and protect. Adam is told to be on guard against the predator, who was still lurking in the earth, and to protect his authority, rule, and dominion. Satan's time is short. If man walks in the light of God and begins to produce sinless offspring that will begin to populate the worlds, he (Satan) will be locked up immediately. He searches the garden for an ally, something he can use to cause the fall of man. "Adam," says he, "must eat of the tree of the knowledge of good and evil. He must break the stewardship of law that God gave." Satan knows the laws of the universe. "If I can just get Adam to sin, then the world will be mine, and man will become my servant," says he. "To whom ye yield yourselves servants to obey, his servants ye are to whom ye obey." Satan is the father of sin. He was the first to rebel against God's stewardship of law. He knows how to entice to sin. He needs to enact his evil plan, so he begins talking to Adam's subjects. "Now the serpent was more subtle than any beast of the field *which the Lord God had made*. And he said unto the woman, yea hath God said, ye shall not eat of every tree of the garden?" (Genesis 3:1). Satan begins to talk to Adam's help. He convinces the serpent, like he did the fallen angels, that if he came along with his way, he would rule with him in the place of man. Now the serpent had great intellect and was created good and was most valuable to Adam. He had the gift to reason and speak. Most importantly, he possessed will, but after spending time with the master deceiver, he became subtle. *Subtle* in the Hebrew is *aruwm* and means "to be crafty and cunning in a bad sense." The devil who had corrupted his own wisdom now does the same to the serpent. The serpent was made to be an aid to man in administering governance in the garden, so conversation with Adam and Eve was the norm. Satan and the serpent hatched the plan. Satan asked the serpent, "What do you see in Adam that we can use to cause his fall?" The serpent, who is very familiar with them both, said Eve. "She is his heart, and she is the weaker of the two. If we get her to the tree, we can get her to eat of it, and because of Adam's great love for her, she will cause him to eat also." Now every child who has ever attended Sunday School knows what happened. The plan worked, and now Adam has allowed sin into the world. Romans 5:12 laments, "Wherefore, as by one man sin entered into the world, and death by sin; and so death passed upon all men, for that all have sinned." Satan had done it. He had caused God's prize creation to submit to him and therefore reclaim dominion of the earth. Now because of God's great love for man, He will not do to them what He did to the humanoid world that He created them to replace. Then too, God will not allow all His creation to see His plan to populate the worlds nullified by the very angel who destroyed it in the first place. God now pronounces judgment upon this social system and passes His divine sentence upon them. To the serpent, God says, "Thou art cursed above all cattle, and above every beast of the field; upon thy belly shalt thou go, and dust shalt thou eat all the days of thy life." Please understand that it would be wrong for God to penalize the serpent if the serpent was not a willing participant in the fall. I have heard it said that Satan became a serpent and carried out the deception, but this is not what the Bible articulates. It was a beast of the field, and unfortunately for the serpent, he aligned his will with the will of the devil. Eve was punished for her part in the deception. She would bring forth her children in pain and travail, and she would be ruled by her husband. The serpent's punishment of losing his limbs and the power of speech and the woman's punishment of sorrow in childbearing cannot compare to the judgment pronounced on the man. The earth, which was restored to a wonderful paradise and yielded forth plenty, was now under a curse. The earth did nothing wrong, but because its covering and light had fallen under the control of Satan, it too now would be under its wicked control. "Cursed is the ground for thy sake; in sorrow shalt thou eat of it all the days of thy life; Thorns also and thistles shall it bring forth to thee; and thou shalt eat the herb of the field" (Genesis 3:17–18). The judgment of thorns upon the earth symbolize the desolation and famines that would come on the earth because of man. Now, many have blamed God for this, but again we must remember, God's creations are perfect when He first creates. Here we see the truth of the matter: because of Adam breaking God's law, now the earth is under the curse. Thistles were poisonous weeds that corrupted all good vegetation and had no place on the world until the fall of Adam. All these hardships, man was not to know, and as terrible as they were, they were nothing compared to the judgment God pronounced next. "In the sweat of thy face shalt thou eat bread, till thy return unto the ground; for out of it wast thou taken: for dust thou art, and unto dust shalt thou return" (Genesis 3:19). The terror of knowing that you are going to die is perhaps the greatest fear a person can face, but can you imagine how Adam must have felt? He received the plan of God to rule and have dominion on earth and the stars and to fulfill the glorious plan of God. But now, *you will die,*

THE AGE OF AGES AND THE CHRISTIAN'S FUTURE

and all humanity will die because of you!" Satan had now become the *god of this world.* Second Corinthians 4:34 laments,

> But if our gospel be hid, it is hid to them that are lost; in whom *the god of this world* (social system) hath blinded the minds of them which believe not, lest the light of the glorious gospel of Christ, who is the image of God, should shine unto them.

Authority and dominion had transferred from Adam to Satan. No one is happy about this wicked development. No, not the Godhead nor the Holy angels, not the countless societies in the heavens, and certainly not the earth and the other fallen worlds who were waiting on the glory of God to be manifested in them by God's replica of Himself—man!

> For even the whole creation, all nature waits eagerly for *the children of God to be revealed* for the creation was subjected to frustration and futility, not willingly because of some intentional fault on its part, but by the will of him who subjected it in hope that the creation itself will also be freed from its bondage and decay, and gain entrance into the *glorious freedom of the children of God.* For we know that the whole creation has been moaning together as in the pains of childbirth until now. (Romans 8:19–22, Amplified)

Notice that just as the earth and all creation is now under the curse because of a man, so too will all creation be liberated by man. What is this *glorious freedom* that the *children of God* will manifest? It will be the power to unlock all fallen creation and realize the full plan of God. We will reveal more of this truth later. For now, Satan's intervention has put a hold on God's plans to restore completely this part of His fallen kingdom. What is the Elohim to do? Will they allow one of their created beings to stop their plan to bring full restoration to the universe? Has Satan outsmarted Elohim and, thus, legally cancelled out his own sentence of death and imprisonment in hell? All of creation is waiting in anticipation. What will God do next?

CHAPTER 5

The Protevangelium

We have seen the judgments of God on the serpent, the woman, and the man, but what about Satan? He is now in charge of the earth again through his manipulation of the serpent, and it appears that he is untouchable. He knows the laws of the Elohim, "To whom ye yield yourselves servants to obey, his servants ye are to whom ye obey." He has caused God's replica of Himself to become a sinner, and, therefore, he has tied the hands of God. Satan exclaims, "There will be no replacement for me. I won't go down to hell to the sides of the pit. I have defeated the plan of God. He can't move against me without moving against my subjects, and man is my subject!" Satan was correct in his assessment about God honoring His law, but as always is the case with him in his dealings with God, he is utterly wrong about his fate. *Know this*, if God makes a judgment about anything, it must and will come to pass. "Yet thou shalt be brought down to hell, to the sides of the pit" is God's judgment upon Satan, and it is surely going to happen! I have noticed in scripture a unique way in which God speaks to Satan. To those who are unaware of this method, it would appear that there in the garden where the mighty Elohim was passing out judgments on the violators of His law, that nothing was pronounced upon Satan. On the contrary, God spoke clearly to him in the language of double reference in Genesis 3:15. The law of double reference in scripture occurs when a visible creature is addressed, but certain statements also refer to an invisible person who is using the visible creature as a tool. Interpreting which statements apply to each person is to associate what could only refer to him. For example, "I will put enmity between thee and the woman, and between thy seed and her seed." This could apply to both the serpent and to Satan, but the last part of verse 15 could only refer to Satan and the Christ. "It shall bruise thy head, and thy shalt bruise his heel." This is the pronouncement of Satan's defeat by the man who was coming to totally crush him and take back all the authority he had gained from Adam. The bruising of His heel is a reference to the temporary suffering Satan would inflict on Him in His passion to the cross. Here in this wonderful verse, we see God's answer to the devil. You will not stop my plan for man to replace you in the kingdom, and you will not escape the judgment I have reserved for you. Here in Genesis 3:15, we have what Bible scholars call the *protevangelium. Protevangelium* is a compound word of two Greek words: *protos*, which means "first," and *evangelion*, which means "good news" or "gospel." Here in the garden, God makes first mention of the gospel. The Christ is coming to take back the authority and dominion that Adam lost and reinstate the destiny of the children of God. Many have attempted to paint God as this unreasonable tyrant who creates famine and disease with no regard for creation, but nothing could be further from the truth. Right when man failed Him and gave back the authority of earth to the devil, God declares His amazing love and grace to him. I will come as a man for man to pay sin's penalty for man. Mankind failed me on a tree, but I will redeem man on a tree (the cross). "Christ hath redeemed us from the curse of the law, being made a curse for us; for it is written, cursed is everyone that hangeth on a tree" (Galatians 3:13). All of creation, upon hearing the decrees of God, understood what this meant. One of the Elohim would have to become a man to fulfill this declaration. Yes, the sovereign Lord and Creator would have to become a man. All creation hushed. What is this love and grace toward man? This was not seen with the fallen angels and the humanoid worlds that sinned! Satan now knows the extent of God's love for man and the Elohim's plan for mankind to have dominion over all the works of his hands. Now Satan knows that mankind are his legal subjects because all mankind is in Adam, and Adam is a sinner. He also knows that if there was a human from humanity who was born without sin and that could live a life without sin that he could atone for all of humanity's sins. Satan worried at the declaration of God in the garden, for he knew that he would not be facing a replica of God but God Himself in human flesh!

CHAPTER 6

The Christ

> When in God's plan the proper time had fully come, God sent
> his son, born of a woman, born under the regulations of the law,
> so that He might redeem and liberate those who were under
> the law, that we who believe might be adopted as sons as God's
> children with all rights as fully grown members of a family.
>
> —Galatians 4:4–5 (Amplified)

The declaration that God made in the garden concerning the human incarnation of one of the members of the Elohim is now upon Satan. He had attempted to stop the life of Christ by inspiring one of his most loyal tools—Herod the Great, the son of Antipater, king of Judea—to kill every male child two years old and under, according to the time which he had inquired of the wise men that the Christ should be born. However, he failed, for God was with Mary and Joseph and by many supernatural events God preserved them and the Christ child. All of creation know what is at stake. Will the plan of God succeed? Will mankind take their rightful place in the family of God, or will Satan defeat the plan of God? The Elohim decides that the God known as the Word would come in the flesh to complete this mission.

In the beginning before all time was the Word
(Christ) and the Word was with God, and the

Word was God Himself. He was continually
existing in the beginning co-eternally with God.
All things were made and came into existence
through Him; and without Him not even one
thing was made that has come into being. (John
1:1–3, Amplified)

And the Word (Christ) became flesh, and lived
among us; and we actually saw His glory, glory as
belongs to the One and only begotten son of the
Father, the Son who is truly unique, the only One
of His kind, who is full of grace and truth absolutely free of deception. (John 1:14, Amplified)

God sought out a young virgin to carry the babe so He could be
a legal advocate on behalf of humanity. "Mary thou shalt conceive in
thy womb, and bring forth a son, and shalt call His name Jesus." *Jesus*
is the Greek form of the Hebrew name *Yehoshua*, which means "God
who is salvation!" As a matter of fact, all the names attributed to Jesus
point to His deity and the performance of the plan of God He is to
complete! *Immanuel* in Matthew 1:23 means "God with us." *Christ*
is from the Greek word *christos* and literally means the consecrated
anointed one. *Jesus Christ*, therefore, means "God with us anointed
to carry out the work of redemption." *Son of man* is a term Jesus
used of Himself in the gospels and refers to His human lineage of
coming from Abraham so He could legally atone for humanity. And
of course, John the Baptist declared of Him in John 1:29, "Behold
the *Lamb of God* which taketh away the sin of the world." This name
instills great fear in the devil, for it points to his loss of control upon
mankind. It refers to Jesus being the sacrifice and atonement for all
mankind by paying sin's penalty. If the Christ can succeed, then the
curse of sin would be broken. King of Kings and Lord of Lords indicates that He is King over all other kings and Lord over all other
lords, all of which receive their authority from Him! The Christ in
the earth is a great concern to the devil. This is not a replica; this is
God in a human body. As His name indicates, He has come on a

mission. He has come to restore humanity and to fulfill the plan of the Elohim in repopulating the worlds. Satan must stop Him, and Christ knows that there will be many encounters with His adversary.

> Then was Jesus led up of the Spirit into the wilderness to be tempted of the devil. And when he had fasted forty days and forty nights, He was afterward an hungred. And when the tempter came to Him, He said, if thou be the Son of God, command that these stones be made bread. But He answered and said, it is written, man shall not live by bread alone, but by every Word that proceedeth out of the mouth of God. Then the devil taketh him up into the Holy City, and setteth Him on a pinnacle of the temple, and saith unto Him If thou be the Son of God, cast thyself down: for it is written He shall give His angels charge concerning thee: and in their hands they shall bear thee up, lest at any time thou dash thy foot against a stone. Jesus said unto him, it is written again, thou shalt not tempt the Lord thy God. Again, the devil taketh Him up into an exceeding high mountain, and sheweth Him all the kingdoms of the world, and the Glory of them; And saith unto Him, all these things will I give thee, if thou wilt fall down and worship me. Then saith Jesus unto him, get thee hence Satan: for it is written, thou shalt worship the Lord thy God, and Him only shalt thou serve. Then the devil leaveth Him, and, behold, angels came and ministered unto him. (Matthew 4:1–11)

The contest has begun. In this corner, the deceiving, cunning usurper of authority and god of this world—Satan, the dragon and that old devil. And in this corner, the Creator of all things, the King of Kings, the Lord of Lords, the Savior, the Alpha and Omega, the conquering Lion of Judah, the Author and Finisher of faith—Jesus the Christ. As we can see, Jesus has to undergo this test. The Spirit of God mandates it. He will lead Him into the conflict and enable Him to defeat the devil. Satan had defeated Adam by using the serpent, but in this conflict, He—the devil himself—would physically and in person do battle with Jesus. Satan does everything in his power to cause Jesus to obey him but to no avail. In fact, the Greek word for tempted is *peirazo* and means "to scrutinize and entice through examination." This evil examination of the Christ not only failed but established the authority of Jesus over the devil moving forward. Jesus served notice to the devil: "I have come to complete the plan of the Elohim, and there is absolutely nothing you can do about it."

CHAPTER 7

Christ's Victory for Man

(Colossians 1:13)

After Jesus the Christ's victory over Satan in their first encounter, the Lord begins to lay the groundwork for the kingdom from the heavens. He has come to introduce the order and rule of God to this fallen part of God's universe. Satan cannot stop the plan of God nor its executor. All of God's righteous creation is in awe of the wonderful plan of God and the amazing love and grace shown toward man. Jesus "begins to preach and to say, Repent: for the kingdom of heaven is at hand" (Matthew 4:17). This strong encouragement to repent by Jesus would mean absolutely nothing if there was no one to whom repentance could be made and a legal remedy for the sin being repented of was accepted. Jesus understands well what the laws of the universe are; He wrote them. One man, Adam, loses dominion and causes death to all. So in order for God's law to be satisfied, it would take another man. Consider Romans 5:12, "Wherefore by *one man* sin entered into the world, and death by sin; and so death passed upon all men, for that all have sinned," and Romans 5:15, "But not as the offence, so also is the free gift. For if through the offence of one many be dead, much more the grace of God, and the gift by grace, which is by one man, Jesus Christ, hath abounded unto many." Jesus is asking for repentance because He knows He's the man to satisfy its requirements. He alone is the way, the truth, and the life. He alone will defeat sin in a human body and, therefore, be a legal and just sacrifice for the sins of the whole world. Death gets its power from sin. Satan had failed to cause Him to sin like Adam. Jesus knows that if He sins, He will die; but if He defeats sin, He will gain immortality for all mankind. He can pay sin's penalty because He has no sin. God can use Him as a scapegoat for humanity. Death cannot legally hold Him because He did no personal sin Himself. "The soul that sinneth, it shall die," the law of God has proclaimed, but He can perform the act of atonement because He is sinless. You see, if He had sinned, then He could not be raised from the dead and, therefore, break death's stranglehold on mankind. Jesus can make the demand for repentance. He alone gives our repentance weight because through His cross, we obtain what our repentance is asking for—forgiveness and deliverance of sin. Jesus was "in all points tempted like as we are, yet without sin." He totally and completely defeated sin in His human body. He now can produce eternal life to all who repent. The sting of death is sin, but Jesus has dealt with it once and for all. "O death, where is thy sting? O grave, where is thy victory?" Death is swallowed up by the victorious life of the Son of God. All who accept Jesus through repentance now have admittance into the kingdom of heaven. He has come from the heavens to put down the kingdom of Satan with all its sin and death. Man no longer has to suffer the eternal effects of its father Adam, for the Christ has come. Let all repent and live, for the glorious establishment of the plan of God has been reasserted into the world.

CHAPTER 8

The Cross

Jesus is a big problem to the devil. Wherever He goes, He exercises mastery over him and his demonic forces, healing the sick, and even raising the dead. Even though he hates Jesus with every ounce of his being, Satan knows that he is still the god of this world. "Jesus," says the devil, "is an annoyance, but I can still enforce my law of sin and death upon the whole world. What can the Christ do to stop me from doing this? Mankind is under my administration and my jurisdiction." Still, he is looking for ways to get rid of Jesus. Jesus is God, but He is also man. "Maybe I can kill Him," Satan shouts, "but how?"

"We can't get him to sin. We've tried over and over, but Jesus is just too holy, too powerful. He toys with us before the people and then dismisses us by rebuke," says the devil's agents. Satan is mad in his hatred toward Jesus. He is determined to kill the Christ. Doesn't he know that "the Son of Man must be delivered into the hands of sinful men and be crucified, and the third day rise again?" Satan knows the law and the scripture, but because he has spent his whole existence twisting and undermining the scripture, he still believes he can change the outcome of it. "Once I kill Him, I will claim Him in the underworld forever," he mused. Satan begins his devious plan. "Judas, the disciple, reminds us of the serpent. Let's begin working on him."

Then entered Satan into Judas surnamed Iscariot,
being of the number of the twelve. And he went

his way, and communed with the chief priests and captains, how he might betray him unto them. (Luke 22:3–4)

How long Satan's evil spirits had been flowing into the mind of this disciple is not known, but like any other being, serpent or humanoid, spending time under his cunning and deception is a deadly proposition. The princes of this world are going to kill Jesus. The devil is making a huge mistake. Scripture suggest that had he and his agents known what the repercussions would be, "they would not have crucified the Lord of Glory." Jesus, on the other hand, is ready to claim the world back for mankind. "Now is the judgment of this world; now shall the prince of this world be cast out." *Judgment* here in the Greek is *krisis* and means "a condemnation through a judicial proceeding." The devil is about to be condemned and his rule and authority over humanity cancelled legally by the death of the Christ on the cross. Satan's intense hatred has clouded his judgment. Not only will he kill Jesus, but he wants Him to suffer greatly. "I'll have my subjects crucify Him." Crucifixion was quite painful. The person was nailed to a cross with each hand stretched as far as they could go, and their feet were nailed together on the bottom post. The cross would then be lifted and violently dropped in a hole that would hold it erect. This alone would cause the disjoining of the body. The person would hang there by the nails until they died. It was sadistic and horrible. It was indeed the very epitome of the curse: "Christ hath redeemed us from the curse of the law, being made a curse for us: for it is written, Cursed is every one that hangeth on a tree" (Galatians 3:13). Jesus had come to do this. He knows that Adam had plunged all humanity into sin and death on a tree and that he would have to atone for all humanity on a tree. Colossians 1:20 states, "And, having made peace through the blood of his cross, *by Him* to reconcile all things unto himself; *by Him*, I say, whether they be things in earth, or things in heaven." Everything will be restored back into right relationship with God because of the wonderful cross of Jesus the Christ, including man's rightful place in the heavens. The new Living Translation of Colossians 2:14–15 states, "He canceled the record of the charges against us and took it away by nailing it to the cross. In this way, he disarmed the spiritual rulers, and authorities. He shamed them publicly by His victory over them on the cross." This wonderful, unspeakable act of redemption by Jesus on the cross has broken forever the curse of sin and its penalty of death! With His life, Jesus has broken Satan's stronghold on mankind. Now, whosoever will can claim the life of Christ as their own and be granted entrance into the kingdom of God. All of creation is witness. They all watched and celebrated the love and grace of the Elohim. He has paid the ransom. The legal requirement of the universe has been met. Man will be eternal again. He will now be able to take his place among God's righteous creation in the heavens!

CHAPTER 9

Resurrection and Ascension

(Acts 2:24)

All the heavenly host is witness to the victory of the Christ on the cross. They saw that the sins of the entire world were heaped upon Him and that He became the sacrificial lamb for all mankind. Satan is devastated. He has but one more card to play. I will not allow Jesus to be resurrected from the dead. "Death, you must hold Him," but death cannot hold one who has never sinned. So after three full days and three full nights, after all legalities of the redemption had been fully paid, the Elohim's other two members, the Father and the Holy Ghost, resurrected Him from the dead.

> But now as things really are Christ has in fact been raised from the dead, and He became the first fruits that is, the first to be resurrected with an incorruptible, immortal body, foreshadowing the resurrection of those who have fallen asleep in death. For since it was by a man that death came into the world, it is also by a Man that the resurrection of the dead has come. (1 Corinthians 15:20–21, Amplified)

The resurrection of Jesus Christ not only meant that the penalty for sin had been legally paid, but it also meant that God would have an immortal man to rule the worlds. Jesus is the first human to possess an immortal body, one that would never die. Not since before the fall of Adam had humanity ruled over death, but now every human being, man or woman, who repents and accepts the Lord Jesus, will never die. We will receive a godlike, gloried immortal body just like the Christ. "Beloved, now are we the sons of God, and it doth not yet appear what we shall be: but we know that, when he (Jesus) shall appear, *we shall be like him*; for we shall see him as he is" (1 John 3:2). Thank You, Lord, for providing us with the God body we will need to fulfill your awesome plan for us. Jesus, after fulfilling the Elohim's prophecy in the Garden of Eden by totally defeating Satan, now goes back to the planet heaven where He ruled from initially; but this time, He is not alone. All the believers who died in the faith—whose mortal bodies the grave claimed—that were forced to go to the underworld located in the center of the earth, were liberated by Him.

> Therefore, it says when he ascended on High, *He led captivity* captive, and he bestowed gifts on men. Now this expression, He ascended, what does it mean except that He also descended from the heights of heaven into the lower parts of the earth? He who descended is the very same as He who also has ascended high above all the heavens, that He might fill all things that is, the whole universe. (Ephesians 4:8–10)

If we examine what this verse tells us about Christ, we see that not only did He go to hell, but He brought all who were believing in His redemption out of hell and took them to heaven alive. Don't miss the last part: "He might fill all things that is the whole universe." Now, because death has been defeated for the children of God, Christ can place them as immortal beings over His works in the heavens. Now, no child of God will ever have to die again. Jesus promised, "I am the resurrection and the life; He that believeth in me, though He were dead, yet shall He live; and whosoever *liveth* and believeth in me *shall never die*, believest thou this?" Jesus has rescued mankind from the god of this world's administration of sin, death, the grave, and hell.

> Giving thanks to the Father, who has qualified us to share in the inheritance of the saints God's people in the Light. For He has rescued us and has drawn us to Himself from the dominion of darkness, and has transferred us to the kingdom of His beloved Son. (Colossians 1:12–13, Amplified)

Now, anyone who can repent can be included in this glorious inheritance and leave this present dominion of darkness. Jesus has done what the Elohim had determined back in the garden when mankind fell. He has risen and completed the work of the redemption.

CHAPTER 10

The Kingdom

(Matthew 6:10)

The judicial proceeding has been done and the sentence now pronounced on the rule of Satan in the world. Now, time is taken for the judgment to be enacted. The devil now knows that his time is short and that he can no longer hold mankind because of the work of Jesus Christ. The devil decides, "I'm going to stop the message of the kingdom and cause as many as I can to miss it." You wonder why there are so many religions and philosophies? The reason is the great deceiver. He must distort the gospel of the kingdom. Satan says, "Man must not know the full extent of my defeat. I will blind their minds and use the things of my now-defeated kingdom to keep them from the gospel of the kingdom." Misery loves company, and because Satan hates man so much, he wants him to suffer with him, and because the kingdom from the heavens is now in the realm of profession—meaning, the kingdom is a matter of fact, and it will be established. However, now it is not fully realized in the earth. Meanwhile, Satan has time to damn as many souls as he can. God, knowing the need for the world to know the truth about the blessing of the kingdom, establishes the church. Jesus chose twelve men to carry out His mission. The message that He is risen and what that meant is fully communicated. Jesus said, "This good news of the kingdom (the gospel) will be preached throughout the whole world as a testimony to all the nations, and then the end (of the age) will come" (Matthew 24:14, Amplified). The full gospel is what the early church understood. They know exactly what Jesus meant when He said, "Repent for the kingdom of heaven is at hand." They knew that God was about to restore this fallen part of the universe and cancel sin and death's claim on humanity. There will be no death in the heavens where mankind is to rule. There will be no colonization on the planets by sinful man. God will not allow death on His worlds. Yes, it is in the DNA of man to explore the stars because he was created to rule them, but no matter how many rockets or satellites we send to space, the universe will not be accessible. God alone will determine what immortal child of God will rule in the stars. Satan attempting to colonize the heavens is a desperate and feeble attempt to undermine the plan of God. He and his angels have already been publicly defeated. The devil has lost his control of the earth, and his angels have lost their rights to the planets that they once ruled in the dispensation of angels in the dateless past as well. They cannot establish their dominion in the stars because Jesus has disarmed all spiritual rulers and authorities. Know this, because the kingdom of God is in the realm of profession, Satan still has control through the *kosmos*. *Kosmos* is the Greek word for world and means the social system. As it relates to Satan's authority, it means the order, behavior, fashion and government of this world system and the things that make up its evil and rebellion against God. Consider James 4:4: "Ye adulterers and adulteresses, know ye not that the friendship of the world is enmity with God? whosoever therefore will be a friend of the world is the enemy of God." This is not referring to the earth itself but to the social system instituted by Satan who is called "the god of this world." In 2 Corinthians 4:3–4, the devil has had thousands of years to ingrain his evil social system upon man. All his evil deceptions and inventions are rapidly growing in the world even now. So it is on one hand, this present evil social system inspired and propagated by Satan against the kingdom of God from the heavens. At stake are the future of mankind and the very souls of men. I want you to understand completely, without a doubt in your mind, that the kingdom is here and is right now represented by the church. "Thy kingdom come" is a fact. It is a reality, and there's nothing any creature can do to stop it. This social order under the devil is about to end. Galatians 1:3–4 states, "Grace be to you and peace from God the Father, and from our Lord Jesus Christ, who gave Himself for our sins, that He might deliver us from *this present evil world.*" The only thing Satan and his forces can do now is produce deceptions and falsehoods to keep mankind away from Jesus Christ and the glorious kingdom He came to provide!

CHAPTER 11

❦

The Mystery of Iniquity

For the mystery of iniquity doth already work; only He who
now letteth will let, until he be taken out of the way.

—2 Thessalonians 2:7

When we look closer with the mind of the Spirit, we can see that
there is a clandestine working by Satan through the *kosmos* to
move humanity further away from Christ, God, and the things that
bring mankind into salvation. The Bible calls this evil moving of
Satan *the mystery of iniquity*. The secret workings of Satan in the last
days are producing some strange and mysterious phenomena. For
example, we see sinkholes and earthquakes, tornados and hurricanes,
and other disasters that are too numerous to list. Signs in the heavens and unexplained events that boggle the mind in addition to the
shift in cultural norms indicate to us the speed of the devil's wicked
agenda.

When we examine the word *mystery* in the Scriptures, the Greek
translation is from the word *musterion*, which has two distinct inter-
pretations. The first interpretation means *a secret*, which is being outside the range of unassisted natural apprehension that can be made
known *only* by divine revelation (that which must be revealed by
God to be fully understood). This first meaning of *mystery* is also
why the organized system of the devil cannot be seen by those who

are of the world. Second Corinthians 4:4 reminds us that "the god of this world hath blinded the minds of them which believe not." Yes, Satan is keeping the "light of the glorious gospel of Christ" hidden from humanity! The good news is that the Christian has been given a special discerning that 1 John 2:20 calls an *unction*. "We know all things," and with this sight of the Holy Spirit, we can see what others do not.

The second interpretation of *musterion* means to *shut the mouth through silence imposed by initiation*, whether through religious entities, fraternities, sororities, or any other secret organization. Looking at this second meaning of the word *mystery* through the prism of scripture, we see that the devil has had many secret organizations and societies that are working against the kingdom of heaven. Satanic cults, alternate societies, clubs, and other secret orders are in the land today, and they are working in concert with the forces of darkness. True Christians are not fooled by the camaraderie and unity of such organizations, nor are they deceived by the so-called "good works" done by them. Isaiah 64:6 reminds us, "We are ALL infected and impure with sin" (New Living Translation). "When we display our righteous deeds, they are nothing but filthy rags." Anything that does *not* originate from Christ is of the world. Reader, beware that Satan often points to the good of mankind as an alternative to the sin-atoning, *all*-powerful work of Jesus Christ. Secret organizations are forbidden by God. Consider Ephesians 5: 11–12: "And have no fellowship with the unfruitful works of darkness, but rather reprove them for it is a shame even to speak of those things which are done of them in secret."

The Greek word for iniquity is *anomia*, and it simply means "illegality" or "a violation of law or unrighteous behavior." Some of the secret rites of ancient societies were so wicked that they could only be performed in the dark of night. History tells us that the secret organizations of Eleusinian and bacchanalian mysteries were so immoral and abominable that they were outlawed and banished by the Roman senate. That same evil working on humanity is alive and advancing all over the world. Humanity is receiving an empowerment from evil to deny God and His laws. This is what I call *satanic courage*.

Satanic courage is the *bold* ability to oppose God, the gospel, and the plain *truth* of how He established nature and the right order to all things. Those who exhibit this evil trait think, believe, and act like Satan and side with him in most matters. When you look at the world today, it is obvious that it is out of order with God's Word and His will for humanity. It is especially obvious to the true Spirit-filled child of God. The Bible tells us in 1 John 5:19, "And we know that we are of God and the whole world lieth in wickedness," but the whole world is being deceived by the devil. Governments, nations, organizations, and even so-called *"churches"* are in lockstep with his evil designs.

Satan needs man to break God's laws. He knows he is defeated, and his days are numbered, but he hates God and resents God's replacement for him—*man*. He will destroy as many as he can. He and his evil army are moving in the *kosmos* to produce error and deception with the intent on damning as many souls as they can. This is why *true* Christians adhere to Ephesians 6:11–12:

> Put on the whole armour of God that ye may be able to stand against the wiles of the devil. For we wrestle not against flesh and blood, but against principalities, against power, against the rulers of darkness of this world, against spiritual wickedness in high places.

The Greek word for *wiles* is *methodeias*. These are the different methods, means, plans, and schemes used to deceive, ensnare, entrap, and ruin the souls of men. Again, the Spirit-filled child of God *should* be able to detect these evil wiles, for he is not ignorant of Satan's devices. This present social system is controlled and ordered by devils. They are using everything in this system to hide the glorious gospel of the Lord Jesus Christ. Perhaps the three most effective tools of enabling man to break God's laws and to establish them in satanic courage are entertainment, governments, and so-called "science."

The definition for "entertainment" is the action of providing or being provided with amusement or enjoyment. Evil spirits anoint the actor or entertainer to relax the audience to become more open to the suggestion of sin. This tool plants idea and imagery in the mind of its consumer. This seed is planted and watered over and over until it yields the fruit of conformity or tolerance to the idea. It is designed to cause mankind to lose the will to resist the devil's ideals and behavior and to just accept it and go along with it as normal in society. If one is awake, he can clearly see the hand of Satan in the world's entertainment. It seems the more vile and dysfunctional the entertainer or movie, the more critically acclaimed it becomes. Patrons by the millions await with great anticipation of the latest release of obscenity and vulgarity released by Hollywood. Two men kissing each other was not normal sixty years ago, even though Hollywood says it is normal today. Now I am about to upset some of you who are reading this revelation with what I'm going to say next, but I must reveal the truth of the kingdom. The devil wishes to make homosexuality a normal practice in the world today, but it is a sin of monumental importance. Satan knows that mankind is to repopulate the worlds, and perpetrating a lifestyle where the natural way of procreation is challenged is an offhanded way of insulting God and is right up his evil alley. Satan's agenda is to kill, steal, and destroy. He doesn't want a single human being to be born, for he knows that each one is a potential heir of the wonderful provision of Christ and a painful reminder of his own paradise lost. This is especially the case with male homosexuality. Satan wants to degrade God by causing man, who is made in His image and likeness, to defy the natural way of creation. Man was intended to be holy and a like representative of God to *all* creation. God gives man the woman to love and procreate. The laws of creation was and is "everything after its own kind." A male was to be a male with the same initial feeling and desire for a female and vice versa with the female toward the male. This was how the original law of God in creation worked. It was innate in the DNA of both to have natural desire for the opposite sex to aid them in the replenishing of the earth and worlds. The lie being propagated by devils is that people are born homosexual, and we should all accept that God made them that way. This is not in harmony with the laws of God governing creation. Consider Romans 1:24–27 (NLT).

> So God abandoned them to do whatever shameful things their hearts desired. As a result, they did vile and degrading things with each other's bodies. They traded the truth about God for a lie. So they worshiped and served the things God created instead of the Creator himself, who is worthy of eternal praise! Amen. That is why God abandoned them to their shameful desires. Even the women turned against the natural way to have sex and instead indulged in sex with each other. And the men, instead of having normal sexual relations with women, burned with lust for each other. Men did shameful things with other men, and as a result of this sin, they suffered within themselves the penalty they deserved.

It would be unfair for God to make one homosexual and then punish them into an eternal hell for being what He made them. God's word calls this unnatural lifestyle vile and shameful. We know that God doesn't make *anything* vile and shameful like Satan, the fallen angels, humanoid earthlings, and the serpent; people *become* sinful.

I will now explain how a person believes they are not what God initially created them to be. In the dispensation of angels, when Satan ruled the subjects of the earth in that social system, their disembodied spirits became evil spirits that fell under the authority of the devil. As we pointed out before, in every social system, there is male and female, so in his attempt to hinder God's plan of populating the world, he commands these spirits to inhabit mankind and influences the personality of the demon-influenced person. When one thousand evil spirits dwell in an individual, you better believe that individual will begin to take on the characteristics of those spirits that dwell in them. Male devils in female humans will undoubtedly lead the female to believe she is a man trapped in a female body. The same is true in the case of the male under the influences of female spirits. It is a fact of Scripture that as many as six thousand evil spirits can indwell a human. Consider Jesus's confrontation with a demon-possessed man in Mark 5:2–17 (NLT).

> When Jesus climbed out of the boat, a man possessed by an evil spirit came out from the tombs to meet him. This man lived in the burial caves and could no longer be restrained, even with a chain. Whenever he was put into chains and shackles—as he often was—he snapped the chains from his wrists and smashed the shackles. No one was strong enough to subdue him. Day and night he wandered among the burial caves and in the hills, howling and cutting himself with sharp stones. When Jesus was still some distance away, the man saw him, ran to meet him, and bowed low before him. With a shriek, he screamed, "Why are you interfering with me, Jesus, Son of the Most High God? In the name of God, I beg you, don't torture me!" For Jesus had already said to the spirit, "Come out of the man, you evil spirit." Then Jesus demanded, "What is your name?" And he replied, "My name is Legion, because there are many of us inside this man." Then the evil spirits begged him again and again not to send them to some distant place. There happened to be a large herd of pigs feeding on the hillside nearby. "Send us into those pigs," the spirits begged. "Let us enter them." So Jesus gave them permission. *The evil spirits came out of the man* and entered the pigs, and the entire herd of about 2,000 pigs plunged down the steep hillside into the lake and drowned in the water. The herdsmen fled to the nearby town and the surrounding countryside, spreading the news

as they ran. People rushed out to see what had happened. A crowd soon gathered around Jesus, and they saw the man who had been possessed by the legion of demons. He was sitting there fully clothed and perfectly sane, and they were all afraid. Then those who had seen what happened told the others about the demon-possessed man and the pigs. And the crowd began pleading with Jesus to go away and leave them alone.

Notice that the demon-possessed man was totally controlled in his soul by six thousand demons. Satan's society wants to delegitimize the time-tested and proven method of casting out demons that Christ administered and later delegated to the church. He wants everyone to buy into the lie that they were genetically made that way. There is no gene that causes a man to believe he is a woman. This is a spiritual issue! God doesn't make mistakes, and He certainly doesn't contradict Himself. What God says is *sin is sin*, and God's creational law is right: "everything after its own kind." God loves all people and seeks to deliver all people from their sin. It is not God's love to allow one to die in their sins and go to hell. So if God made you homosexual, you cannot repent from what God made you, and there is no need to be forgiven. This point of view is blasphemy because it depreciates the atoning work of Jesus in dealing with sin, and homosexuality is sin.

In order to be forgiven of any sin, one must first repent, which simply means to turn away from and forsake that missing of the mark. So you see, the one who believes God made him a homosexual is deceived into never receiving forgiveness because there is no point in repenting when God condones him by making him that way. Please know this: if you are struggling with this sin in particular, you can be delivered and set free. Don't believe the lies of Satan! God will save you if you repent. Just like the man possessed by six thousand demons reached Jesus, you too can push past those spirits in your mind, and the real you can cry out to the Savior for help. Jesus loves you, and He shed His own blood on the cross to liberate you from the clutches of Satan. Hollywood is casting its evil spell on the world through TV, movies, and all other venues, but don't accept Satan's lie. God's word is still right. To the believer in the Lord Jesus Christ, I want to say to you, stop opening yourselves up to every suggestion Satan injects into the world through entertainment. I am afraid that some Christians give more time to the influences of evil spirits than they do with the Word of God. We are seeing the influence of Hollywood in the church and the lifestyle of the Christian. When anyone, non-Christian or Christian alike, sit in a movie theater or any other medium used by the devil to propagate his evil morality, he will be injected with it. We wonder how the Christian church can begin to ordain homosexual bishops and clergy in total opposition to God's holy Word. The relaxing of society by the heart-wrenching, emotion-gripping art of entertainment is a major reason why. There are some things that can and should be avoided by the Christian; for all that is holy, I cannot understand how Spirit-filled Christians can sit for hours in a dark theater and watch as actors fornicate, commit adultery, and insult the lord Jesus Christ. Remember God's word in 2 Corinthians 6:14–17 (NLT):

> Don't team up with those who are unbelievers. How can righteousness be a partner with wickedness? How can light live with darkness? What harmony can there be between Christ and the devil? How can a believer be a partner with an unbeliever? And what union can there be between God's temple and idols? For we are the temple of the living God. As God said: "I will live in them and walk among them. I will be their God, and they will be my people. Therefore, come out from among unbelievers, and separate yourselves from them, says the LORD. Don't touch their filthy things, and I will welcome you."

When looking at how Satan is using governments, all one needs to do is look at the laws of the land: legalizing same-sex marriage, abortion, and other "so called laws" that break the commandments of

God. Government is impacted by the climate of society, and because all of the world is being manipulated by the god of this world, all governments are fallen. Politics look at what is trending and what is popular among people in its development of its platform. Even so-called Christian politicians will site what is politically correct over what the Word of God demands, even making iniquity legal. They may believe the separation of church and state is the best way to govern, but this is inaccurate according to God's Word. Never forget that government comes from God. Romans 13:1 says, "Everyone must submit to governing authorities. For all authority comes from God." So Christians understand that God intended to pass down His moral and spiritual laws to humanity by government, but because all governments in the *kosmos* are under Satan's influence, many of the laws are in direct opposition to God's laws.

What do we do about legal laws that break God's laws? As Christians, we keep God's law first! We never break government law willingly, but we must never allow government to cause us to disobey God as He is revealed through His Word. Many of Satan's advocates are assaulting the laws of God and replacing them with human concepts. Have you noticed the demonic effort to remove the Ten Commandments from the courtrooms and justice halls? The perfect law to govern is represented by those tablets of stone written by the finger of God and given to Moses to teach His people. Government is supposed to set the boundaries for what is right and what is wrong, but with Satan at the helm, all authority is in opposition to God and what He has determined in His law to be right or wrong.

True science will always reveal the truth of God's existence and the validity of His Word. Romans 1:20 will be the conclusion to all sincere scientific research. It states, "For ever since the world was created people have seen the earth and sky. Through everything God made, they can clearly see His invisible qualities—His eternal power and divine nature. So they have no excuse for not knowing God." Satan is not interested in the truth. He is the father of lies. He institutes what 1 Timothy 6:20 calls "science falsely so-called"—so-called intelligence that denies the truth of God. These foolish and improbable theories are designed to cause humanity to look someplace else for the meaning of all things instead of to God. Have you noticed that none of their theories that allegedly contradict God's Word can be proven as fact, only conjecture? They believe in the Big Bang Theory and the theory that man evolved from apes and other laughable notions and still have the unmitigated gall to call Christians ignorant and unlearned. Scripture states, "Professing themselves to be wise, they became fools" (Romans 1:22). We as Christians have the light and the truth, so Satan has to deceive the simple with this ridiculous academia and produce as much confusion as he can to hide the truth from man. Also in his evil design is the plan to make mankind feel dumb, stupid, and uneducated if they do not accept this so-called "scientific knowledge." These three tools of iniquity can be spotted easily by Christians, but the deadliest deception to the world that the devil is hatching is hidden in plain sight.

CHAPTER 12

The UFO and Alien Deception

All the world should know that Satan is a deceiver. He has but a short time before the Christ returns and executes the judgment upon him and his unholy social order. He has been using all of the world's mechanisms to guide the social system's thinking, and through his many media strands, he is preparing them for the end of his reign. There is going to be a time when the final war between Satan and his forces and God and His forces will take place. This event will end with Satan and his forces being defeated and finally cast into the prison made for him and his army. Revelation 20:10 tells us, "And the devil that deceived them was cast into the lake of fire and brimstone, where the beast and the false prophet are and shall be tormented day and night for ever and ever." Right now, the devil is creating an army to resist the Elohim. He has been tampering with the human and animal gene pool since the days of Adam. He has been creating monsters to help him in destroying mankind and using their evil assistance to deceive humanity. God does not make monsters to torment humanity. He loves man and has a special place for him in the universe. But monsters do exist! Consider the monsters that are mentioned in Revelation 9:7–11 (NLT):

> The locusts looked like horses prepared for bat-
> tle. They had what looked like gold crowns on
> their heads, and their faces looked like human

faces. They had hair like women's hair and teeth like the teeth of a lion. They wore armor made of iron, and their wings roared like an army of chariots rushing into battle. They had tails that stung like scorpions, and for five months they had the power to torment people. Their king is the angel from the bottomless pit; his name in Hebrew is Abaddon, and in Greek, Apollyon— the Destroyer.

These monsters are presently locked up in the infernal regions of hell and are there because of their sins and allegiance to the devil. Such monstrosities are no doubt the manifestation of a fallen angel who sought to be God and tampered with the gene pool of creation to produce such wicked beings. In the final days, they will be unleashed upon the world with all of the other DNA manipulations of Satan. The mystery of iniquity has been in motion ever since Satan caused the fall of man, and we are seeing it all over the world with the alien and UFO phenomenon.

Looking back at the history of earth, we can see the evil plan of the devil to produce other beings upon it to rival man. If you are really "awake," you can see how the devil is weaving his deceptive plan to cause the whole world to accept these beings. The comic book characters of Marvel and DC Comics are dominating the television and movie landscape; and interestingly, monsters like the Hulk and Wolverine are seen in a sympathetic light. People are rooting for and loving monsters. The tool of entertainment is used to plant their ungodly imagery into the consciousness of the public for the purpose of softening the perception of monsters. Know this: if it is not a man, it cannot be trusted. All other DNA manipulations have their origins from Satan, and they are his manipulations filled with evil spirits. The deception is portraying that which is evil as good and heroic. When Satan's army is fully released upon the world, he will need humanity to accept them. His public relations campaign is already on full display to begin planting the great deception, and the truth of the matter is that they are inherently evil. Since the very beginning, Satan has attempted to produce bullies or tyrants to oppress and enslave humanity. Look at Genesis 6:1–4 (NLT):

> Then the people began to multiply on the earth, and daughters were born to them. The sons of God (Angels) saw the beautiful women and took any they wanted as their wives. Then the LORD said, "My Spirit will not put up with humans for such a long time, for they are only mortal flesh. In the future, their normal lifespan will be no more than 120 years."

In those days, and for some time after, giant Nephilites lived on the earth, for whenever the sons of God (angels) had intercourse with women, they gave birth to children who became the heroes and famous warriors of ancient times. The Hebrew word for "giants" is *nephilim* and means bully, tyrant, or giant. It is from the root Hebrew word *nephal*, which means to fall. This brings us to the phrase "the fallen angels," who father the Nephil. To say that both fallen angels and giants are Nephilim or Nephal would not be accurate. Notice that in the days of Noah, an age upon the earth, the giants filled and corrupted the earth. Josephus, the Jewish historian, wrote concerning this evil period in history,

> Whereby they made God to be their enemy; for many angels of god accompanied with women and begat sons that proved unjust and despisers of all that was good on account of the confidence they had in their own strength, for the tradition is that these men did what resembled the acts of those whom the Grecians call Giants.

It is a fact of Scripture that giants are beings of abnormal size and have lived on earth and will be on the earth in the last days.

It is one of the most fascinating facts of the Bible. Job 16:14 describes the terror of these ungodly creatures: "he breaketh me with breach upon breach, he runneth upon me *like a giant.*"

Deuteronomy 3:1–13 tells us that Og the king of the Amorites was at least eighteen feet tall; his bed was eighteen and one half feet long and eight feet four inches wide. In describing some of the terrible features of these monsters, consider what 2 Samuel 21:20 says: "And there was yet a battle in Gath, where was a man of great stature, that had on every hand six fingers, and on every foot six toes, four and twenty in number; and he also was born to the giant." Numbers 13:33 describes the Anakim; Deuteronomy 2:10 describes the Emim; Deuteronomy 2:19–21 described the Zamzummim. The Kenites, Kenizzites, Kadmonites, Hittites, Perizzites, Rephaims, Amorites, Canaanites, Girgashites, Jebusites, Hivites, Anakim, and Caphtorim were some of the races of giants who filled the whole country, trying to contest God's people's claim on the promised land. The people of God will always be opposed by the DNA manipulations of Satan. These fallen angels leave their own realm and native state assigned to them by God and began to live among men, marrying their daughters, breaking the law of God concerning angels remaining in their own estate. Angels, particularly fallen ones, are not allowed to manifest themselves to humanity without the express permission of God. Jude 6 states, "And the angels which kept not their first estate, but left their own habitation, He hath reserved in everlasting chains under darkness unto the judgment of the great day." Satan's angels also break God's law of creation and reproduction by producing hybrid offspring. God's law of everything after its own kind was now violated by these fallen ones. Satan also knew that if he could corrupt all human flesh, there could be no pure human race to produce the human seed to come and pay sin's penalty for man. The sin of going after strange flesh is one of the chief strategies of Satan in opposing the plan of God.

By this strategy, he can diminish man and build his unholy army. In the Genesis (beginning), Satan uses this design very effectively. He causes all of humanity to become entwined with different types of blood and to accept the social order of bullies and tyrants. The sons of Adam became irrecoverable; the spirit of God cannot reach them; and just like today in some, the work of the flesh was so powerful that they couldn't repent. What it was like to live among the giants and all the other genetically altered beings is a mystery, but what we know is that this will happen again in the last days. We are witnessing the introduction of their return to the earth visibly. Think about the ancient heroes and famous warriors of those days. Hercules, for example, is said to be the son of Zeus (a god) and Alcmene (a human mother), according to Greek mythology. Like most legends and historical myths, there is a noticeable hint of truth to these accounts. Zeus is not God but perhaps a representation of a fallen angel who married a human wife and conceived a Nephilim warrior who performed great feats. The Bible declares that there is no true God besides the Elohim. Throughout earth's history, many fallen angels have declared just like Satan, "I will be like the most high God," and down through the centuries, these tales were passed on. It is of note that most of Hollywood's blockbuster movies involve some type of Nephilim! Back in the time of Noah, God's Word indicates how disappointed He was with humankind. He didn't like how easily they were corrupted in their flesh. The manipulation of the DNA violated the plan and creation of God. Genesis 6:5 declares, "And God saw the wickedness of man was great in the earth. And that every imagination of the thoughts of his heart was only evil continually." With the influence of demon spirits within them and the fallen angels and Nephilim bullies contact among them, their imaginations produced some wicked concepts. Have you ever read about the satyr in Isaiah 13:21? "But wild beasts of the desert shall lie there; and their houses shall be full of doleful creatures; and owls shall dwell there, and satyrs shall dance there." According to Greek mythology, satyrs were male half-man-half-goat creatures who were characterized by their ribaldry and were known for their love of wine, music, dancing, and women. Interestingly, a major physical characteristic of a satyr was exaggerated erection of its sexual organ, which he often attempted to seduce or rape mortal women with. They were known to practice bestiality and other sexually perverse things. Their images were worshipped by ancient people like the Edomites, Canaanites, and others. Such creatures like the *centaur*, who were half man half horse, and the *minotaur*, who were said to have the head of a bull and the body of a man, were but a few of Satan's evil creations. All flesh had corrupted its way upon earth through the sin of strange flesh—angels with women, men with beasts, and many other sexual perversions that are too lengthy to mention. We get a glimpse into their wicked activity by considering God's laws to the Israelites who would be coming into contact with them in Leviticus 18: 22–24 (NLT):

> Do not practice homosexuality, having sex with another man as with a woman. It is a detestable sin. A man must not defile himself by having sex with an animal. And a woman must not offer herself to a male animal to have intercourse with it. This is a perverse act. Do not defile yourselves in any of these ways, for the people I am driving out before you have defiled themselves in *all these ways*.

Satan's goal has always been first to corrupt the seed of man to stop the coming of the Lord Jesus to earth to pay the penalty for sin. Secondly, he wanted to raise a DNA-altered people who would be filled with demon spirits that he could command.

Such genetically manufactured creatures do not have their origin from God and will always oppose the plan of God. This is the main reason God used Israel to totally destroy all Nephilim nations, both male and female, child and aged alike. The law of God would not allow Israel to mix with these nations because they were to carry the pure Adamic seed that would produce the Christ, and they were instructed to totally destroy them and those that fell under their wicked control. God loved the human race so much that He produced a plan to save it and wouldn't allow Satan and his agents to stop it. This is the reason for the flood of Noah and the judgment of Sodom and Gomorrah; both were filled with Nephilim influence. The sin of the fallen angel is mentioned with the sin of Sodom and Gomorrah in 2 Peter 2:4–9 and Jude 6–7. This indicates to us that the sin of strange flesh and the immediate judgment that comes because of it were the cause of their destruction.

Earth is moving closer to this day of wrath. Consider the words of the Lord Jesus Christ in Matthew 24:37 (NLT): "When the Son of Man returns, it will be like it was in Noah's day." Jesus gives us insight to what the social system will be like when He returns to carry out the sentence on the devil. Nephilim and other DNA manipulations will once again be on the earth, the sin of strange flesh will be normal, and continual wickedness will be in the heart of man. Pederasty, bestiality, and other sexually perverted organizations are on the rise. This brings me to *transhumanism*, which is an international, cultural, and intellectual movement with an eventual goal of fundamentally transferring the human condition by developing and making widely available technologies to greatly enhance human intellectual, physical, and psychological capacities. They believe humans may be able to transform themselves into beings with such greatly expanded abilities that they would be considered posthuman, which is a speculative being that reconceives the human into a superman or superwoman. This is Darwinism's great deception and is exactly what the devil promised Adam and Eve in the garden when he said, "Ye shall be as gods." This society adheres to the demonic concept of immortalism. Immortalism is a moral ideology based upon the belief that radical life extension and technological immortality is possible and desirable through research and development. Attempting to achieve immortality any other way than through Christ is an open attack on the sovereign work of God in obtaining immortality for *all*. It attempts to live forever in its same sinful, fallen condition. This is unacceptable to God and the universe, who will have all men to repent and receive the prince of life—the Lord Jesus. Along with these satanic pursuits of immortalism is the social philosophy of *postgenderism*, which seeks the voluntary elimination of gender in humanity. All these satanic tools to stop the procreation of man are at work in the earth today, but the most revealing tell to the days of Noah is the practice of *transgenics*. Transgenics is the transfer of genetic material from one species to another. They engineer genetically modified organisms (GMOs) in their quest to produce different life forms. Captain America is a product of GMOs. Spiderman and other comic book heroes are as well, but are there any real, tangible creations from these genetic engineering techniques? Yes, there are! The

Umbuku lizard, a rare species of lizard living in Africa, which, once altered, had the ability to fly. Currently, there are six flying Umbuku reported to have been created. The lemur cat is a cross between a cat and a lemur. Scientists have created sheep that have human hearts and livers and pigs born with human blood. They injected human brain cells into the brains of rodent fetuses, resulting in the birth of mice with both human and rodent brain cells. The most intriguing is the fern spider. A cross of plant and animal GMOs, the fern spider is a cross between a species of tarantula and the ponga fern. The purpose for such a concoction is to study how spiders with camouflage devices built in fair to spiders without camouflage. Again, all science in Satan's social system is directed by him to hatch his evil designs. The antediluvian age is an example. The devil is producing hybrid beings and fallen angelic technology in plain earthly site. Satan always sought to have representatives on the earth that would be demon controlled so he could achieve pure evil on earth. He has tampered with DNA and other aspects of creation to produce bodies to house the devils from the dateless past. Aliens are the manipulation of Satan and fallen angels of the human, animal, and fallen angel gene pool.

Because of the law of God imposed upon angels who leave their own estate and habitation (Jude 6–7), angels no longer take the daughters of men to wife and produce this satanic offspring, but their objective is carried out in an equally sinister fashion. There are over five million people worldwide who claim to have been abducted by aliens. While we must admit, there are countless *frauds* and *crackpots* who make such assumptions, it does not discredit those who have had authentic encounters. What are we to make of the Apollo astronauts Edgar Mitchell, Gordon Cooper, James Lovell, Frank Borman, Walter Schirra, Neil Armstrong, Buzz Aldrin, Eugene Cernan, and John Blaha, who are on public record as seeing UFOs and, in some cases, aliens? These are brilliant men and America's best. What about the vast number of sightings reported by navy and air force pilots that are so frequent now that the Pentagon had to write new codes on how to engage and report them? These men obviously have the right stuff! Furthermore, how about the many cattle mutilations where brains and hearts and other limbs were surgically removed without the presence of exit wounds? Who could do this and with what technology did he use?

Why does he need the body parts of animals? It is reported that DNA, blood, and other things are taken from human abductees and often reported that the female abductees are impregnated and later reabducted to remove the fetuses. Many report mind-control devices used to impair their memory, and only under deep hypnosis do they recall their ordeal.

Many have reported *three* main types of hybrid Nephilim that masquerade as aliens from other universes. First, the Grays, which is the most common, are between three to four feet tall with huge heads and eyes and have a gray skin color. Second, the Nordics—or Pleiadians, as they are sometimes called—are six feet tall with blond hair and blue eyes and look like men. The third type, the Reptilians, who vary in size but are scaly and monstrous looking, closely resemble reptiles. Where do these creatures come from? Colossians 1:16 says, "All things were created by Him and for Him," but this must be understood to mean the creation of all things in the beginning as He made them and *not* the monstrosities developed by Satan and his agents here on earth. It is true that Satan does not have creative power, but he does have knowledge to manipulate DNA. One thing is for certain: God did *not* make beings to come and kidnap people, destroy livestock, and operate in such an evil and clandestine way. Satan seeks to deceive the world into believing demons are aliens from out of space. Through sorcery and transhumanist technologies, he is producing hybrid bodies for his devils to live in. He is attempting to legitimize the entrance of his agents into the world by having them masquerade as aliens from another universe who come to share the secrets of the origin of life. They will try to convince people that they planted mankind here, and they have returned at the command of God and the Messiah to take humanity to the next level of enlightenment, but they're really Satan and the devils' Antichrist. Now, consider what 2 Thessalonians 2:9–12 says:

> Even him, whose coming is after the working of
> Satan with all power and signs and lying wonders,

> And with all deceivableness of unrighteousness in them that perish; because they received not the love of the truth, that they might be saved. And for this cause God shall send them strong delusion, that they should believe a lie: That they all might be damned who believed not the truth, but had pleasure in unrighteousness.

This is the "lying wonders" strategy of Satan that will cause strong delusion to come upon the world. *Lying wonder* in Greek is *pseudos* and means "a wonder calculated to deceive; to make something appear to be something else by falsehood." This is precisely what the alien and UFO phenomenon is doing. After all, how do you explain their presence in the earth? They are not in unity with the Elohim, and right now, they have not fully revealed themselves to humanity. They do, however, have a time when they will be revealed to the whole world; but for now, God is withholding the evil deception of Satan. Second Thessalonians 2: 6–7 states, "And now ye know what withholdeth that he might be revealed in his time. For the mystery of iniquity doth already work: only he who now letteth will let, until he be taken out of the way." The lie is already working, but the full manifestation of it cannot come until the church is taken up into glory. Then the whole world will be thrust into an age of wonder, when millions of Christians disappear from the face of the earth. All the world will marvel at this time at the appearance of aliens and other life-forms who will suddenly come to the rescue of a bewildered mankind to solve all their riddles and offer them answers in this time of great apprehension. "What happened to all those missing Christians?" the nations will ask, to which the aliens will answer that "another alien force has taken them away, and we are here to offer our help to the rest of you earthlings. They will return again, and we will help you prepare to resist them." Yes, the Lord will return again; and yes, there will be a battle, and most, if not all of the world, will be deceived into fighting against Him. Second Thessalonians 2:8 tells us, "And then shall that wicked be revealed, whom the Lord shall consume with the spirit of His mouth, and shall destroy with the brightness of His coming." All of Satan's designs will be on full display; monsters, giants, and aliens will all be working in concert to produce lying wonders to propagate the father of lies' great deception upon mankind. Strong delusion will be upon the entire earth, and fallen angel technology will be completely released into the world.

If we look closer at the technology in the world, we can see glimpses of this angelic intelligence through genetics and microbiology; robotics; nanotechnologies; and of course, artificial intelligence or AI. AI is the intelligence exhibited by machines or software. This technology seeks to blur the distinction between man and machine. It also seeks to merge the human thought and personality with computer software by using BCIs or brain-computer interfaces. The Chinese seem to be miles ahead in this technology. They have, for public consumption, the hair cloud smart TV, where the watcher controls the functions on it with his brain waves, which are channeled through a mind-set drive on his head. This AI technology brings to mind the scripture in Revelation 13:15: "And he had power to give life unto the image of the beast, that the image of the beast should both speak, and cause that as many as would not worship the image of the beast should be killed." These talking AIs are but a sample of this fallen angel technology. Interestingly, the FDA has approved for consumer consumption the bionic eye, which gives its operator superhuman vision. Bionic muscles and limbs are said to be one hundred times stronger than regular human ones. The ultimate design of robots is to one day be able to download the human soul into this robotic body, thus creating immortality. Many transhumanists believe in the compatibility of human minds with computer hardware, with the theoretical implication that human consciousness may someday be transferred to alternative media, which is a speculative technique commonly known as mind uploading. Yes, technology and sorcery are closely interwoven in transhumanist technologies because they seek to animate machines and objects through human soul and spirit transfer. This is the same magic being used by Satan to animate aliens. Spiritualism is the devil's main tool for his devils to inhabit his hybrid bodies.

In the case of aliens, their bodies are manufactured to deceive man into believing they are from another place. Think about it; if they have come to aid and enlighten humanity, why don't they do it already? Wars, famines, crime, hurricanes, and other hurtful things are plaguing mankind, and they stand by idly and watch the suffering? You know why they can't help? Because they are inherently evil, and as we have already mentioned, they cannot fully reveal themselves until "he be taken out of the way." Then they will be released upon the whole world. I must also note that Satan has human agents on earth who help release these evil manifestations. The Luciferians, the Illuminati, witches, and other sorcerers pray and chant for their wicked appearance and fellowship. Sadly, they are scientists, doctors, bankers, military leaders, and some are involved in the highest levels of government all over the world. Truly, "the whole world lieth in wickedness." UFOs are without a doubt fallen angel technology. The fact that Satan is the author of this deceptive invention and technology can be seen in Ezekiel 28:12: "thou sealest up the sum, full of wisdom, and perfect in beauty." The Hebrew word for wisdom is *chokmah* and refers to technical skills or special abilities in fashioning something. The same word is found in Exodus 35:31: "And he hath filled him with the spirit of God, in wisdom [*chokmah*], in understanding, and in knowledge, and in all manner of workmanship." This shows Satan's special ability to build and produce workmanship. It is the devil's natural character to build and produce technological works, and because these strange crafts are appearing in our habitation, we know he is responsible. Remember God's laws concerning angels and all creation remaining in their own habitation and dimension. Foreign entities cannot come into earth's realm without God's express permission. Life in the universe is governed by God, and that which applies to earth is only for the earth. Satan and his forces are regulated to earth, and God's laws do *not* allow any other heavenly beings to violate His laws of dimensional and universal boundaries. It is true that they are out there in other universes, but they are under obedience to the sovereign laws of the Elohim and at this present time are spectators to the events on our fallen world. Ephesians 3:10 (NLT) says, "God's purpose in all this was to use the church to display his wisdom in its rich variety to all the unseen rulers and authorities in the heavenly places." Satan and his angels are law breakers, and when some of them left their legal boundaries, they were dealt with by God. Jude 6 (NLT) says, "And I remind you of the angels who did not stay within the limits of authority God gave them but left the place where they belonged. God has kept them securely chained in prisons of darkness, waiting for the great day of judgment." All creation knows their boundaries and knows the penalty of breaking God's laws. Reader, you should now begin to see that these UFOs and so-called alien life-forms are not from the constellation Orion but are manifestations of an evil, deceiving force right here in our own habitation. Satan knows the secrets to what each stone, mineral, or plant can produce and the type of power they can yield. He knows how to produce technologies and engineering and then communicate it down to his agents. The knowledge to split the atom and create a nuclear bomb was his wisdom, and he no doubt will attempt to share with man even more inventions of war to help them destroy themselves. God does not give man the knowledge to destroy and change His creative works. James 3:15 reminds us that this knowledge and "wisdom descendeth not from above, but is earthly, sensual and devilish." The craft that we are seeing have their origin from the mind of Satan. Yes, there is a wisdom that comes from devils, and it is designed to manufacture things that will deceive and steal man's heart away from God. It should be no mystery to the church that these lying wonders are appearing in our realm, and their technology is designed to deceive the world. Now, it must be asked, where are these crafts being made? I believe they are made right here on earth! Many former government agents and workers have testified of secret underground facilities where human and so-called aliens cohabitate and work on different projects together. There seems to be a secret hidden agenda at the higher levels of government, a shadow government that is working in lockstep with the god of this world. I cannot say with one hundred percent certainty, but I wouldn't be surprised if there was an agreement with the satanic cults, governments, and so-called alien entities all over the world to accomplish this great deception. One thing is for sure: it would violate God's law if they were a life-form from outside our universe, and they would be judged immediately by God. Knowing that, they are most likely from right here in our realm. The Bible states in Genesis 3:15 that the genetic offspring of Satan would be in hostile conflict with the seed of the woman, and it is a fact of Scripture that Satan has offspring or those being manufactured by his wiles in the earth today. They are the new Nephilim that are masquerading as aliens from another galaxy.

CHAPTER 13

Satan's Last Stand

Therefore rejoice, ye heavens, and ye that dwell in them.
Woe to the inhabiters of the earth and of the sea! For
the devil is come down unto you, having great wrath,
because he knoweth that he hath but a short time.

—Revelation 12:12

After He (the church) is taken out of the way, the devil will release
his full deception upon the world. Just like the days of Noah,
the social order will be inhabited with Nephilim hybrid beings—
aliens, if you prefer that term. All these will be integrated together to
form the social order's last resistance to the judgment to be carried
out upon it by Christ. The world will be the thing of science fiction
as Satan mobilizes his earth army to oppose the great invaders from
space. Satan will use unclean spirits to inspire ambassadors to perform miracles and convince the kings of the earth that the success of
their future lies in them cooperating with him to stop Christ from
taking over the earth. Judgment has been set, and the second man,
Christ, has reclaimed authority for mankind. What the devil stole
from the first man, Adam, has been restored; and now, the devil's
time is up! Revelation 19:11–21 describes the coming of the Lord to
the earth to defeat Satan and his armies in the battle of Armageddon.
Armageddon is derived from two Hebrew words: *har*, meaning "a

mountain range" or "range of hills," and *megiddo*, meaning "rendez-vous." The two words together, *har-megiddo*, refers to the "hill of meeting." Here, Satan will wait for the return of Christ, who he is expecting to come from heaven and deliver Israel. Because the devil knows prophecy, he expects Christ at the end of the 1,260 days or the last three and a half years of the seven-year tribulation period. He will deceive the nations that join him by convincing them that Christ and His armies are invaders from another universe coming to enslave them.

Can't you see CNN, Fox, and all the other networks announcing the coming alien invasion? The false prophet and the Antichrist will pinpoint the time of their arrival down to the minute. They will be greatly deceived, for the truth of the matter is that Christ is coming to give freedom and liberty to the whole world. The battle will ensue.

> And out of his mouth goeth a sharp sword, that with it he should smite the nations: and he shall rule them with a rod of iron: and he treadeth the winepress of the fierceness and wrath of Almighty God. And he hath on his vesture and on his thigh a name written, KING OF KINGS, AND LORD OF LORDS. (verses 15–16).

The executor of the sentence has come, and Satan will lose his grip on the social order forever. The King of all kings has returned to establish the authority of God upon this fallen part of His kingdom. The devil and all of his agents will be defeated. Revelation 20:1–3 tells us,

> And I saw an angel come down from heaven, having the key of the bottomless pit and a great chain in his hand. And he laid hold on the dragon, that old serpent, which is the Devil, and Satan, and bound him a thousand years, And cast him into the bottomless pit, and shut him up, and

set a seal upon him, that he should deceive the nations no more, till the thousand years should be fulfilled: and after that he must be loosed a little season.

These amazing events mark the reestablishment of the plan of God in having all the worlds under His authority and for man to claim his place with God in the universe. Jesus will lead a company of kings and lords from heaven in the Second Advent to begin the administration of the sons of God. He has gained all authority and dominion on their behalf and now begins their position in the plan of God by leading them in a glorious procession to where their reign will start—the planet Earth!

The kingdom from the heavens has many kings and many lords, and because of Jesus Christ, we will come clothed in white apparel and upon white horses. White signifies that we have been made holy, righteous, and pure and therefore capable and worthy rulers of what lies before us. But notice that for a thousand years, the devil will be imprisoned, and during this time, the nations of this world will have an opportunity to receive the kingdom without his evil influences. For the Christians who have obtained immortality—the kings and lords who return with Christ to establish the kingdom—we will rule and reign with Jesus over all the inhabitants of earth. Revelation 20:6 states, "Blessed and holy is he that hath part in the first resurrection: on such the second death hath no power, but they shall be priests of God and of Christ, and shall reign with him a thousand years." The government of the world will be theocratic—meaning, God will be the supreme civil ruler. We will carry the gospel and the laws of God to the whole world, and all will know and have the opportunity to be a part of the kingdom. From earthly Jerusalem, the Lord Jesus will establish His government. In this amazing time of earth's history, there will be two types of human beings: *mortal and immortal.* Kings and lords who have participated in the first resurrection are immortal and have received the glorified, powerful bodies and inner construct of Jesus Christ. Consider Philippians 3:21: "Who shall change our vile body, that it may be fashioned like unto his glorious body, according to the working whereby he is able even to subdue all things unto himself." It is so worth it to be a faithful, true born-again Christian. The immortal body alone is the price of the great pearl that Jesus spoke about. This glory, with all of its power and ability, is the Christian inheritance. In Luke 20:34–36, Jesus said,

> The children of this world marry, and are given in marriage: But they which shall be accounted worthy to obtain that world, and the resurrection from the dead, neither marry, nor are given in marriage: Neither can they die any more: for they are equal unto the angels; and are the children of God, being the children of the resurrection.

The mortal humans will continue to marry and populate the earth and will live for at least one thousand years. There will be the possibility of sin in this age, so God will have laws to make known His will. It is necessary to have laws to set up standards for free will; otherwise, there would be no need of free will to choose between right and wrong. Remember, these earthly subjects have been under the evil influence of the devil, and many of them will rebel against the rule of Christ in their hearts and openly rebel when the devil is loosed at the end of the one thousand years. Revelation 20:7–10 says,

> And when the thousand years are expired, Satan shall be loosed out of his prison, And shall go out to deceive the nations which are in the four quarters of the earth, Gog, and Magog, to gather them together to battle: the number of whom is as the sand of the sea. And they went up on the breadth of the earth, and compassed the camp of the saints about, and the beloved city: and fire came down from God out of heaven, and devoured them. And the devil that deceived them was cast into the lake of fire and brimstone, where the beast and the false prophet are, and

shall be tormented day and night for ever and ever.

Under the most blessed conditions of divine government and having all the privileges of remaining true and becoming reconciled to God, these nations still align themselves with Satan in his last stand of defiance and hostility toward God. These nations will be judged along with their master and receive the same eternal punishment. There will be no more evil influence upon the earth, and mankind and all the nations that remain true to the divine government of Christ will be permitted to remain and inherit the kingdom.

Jesus declares in Matthew 25:31–34, 41,

> When the Son of man shall come in his glory, and all the holy angels with him, then shall he sit upon the throne of his glory. And before him shall be gathered all nations and he shall separate them one from another, as a shepherd divideth his sheep from the goats. And he shall set the sheep on his right hand, but the goats on the left. Then shall the King say unto them on his right hand, Come, ye blessed of my Father, inherit the kingdom prepared for you from the foundation of the world. Then shall he say also unto them on the left hand, Depart from me, ye cursed, into everlasting fire, prepared for the devil and his angels.

Hallelujah! No more devils; no more wars; no more storms; no more sickness, poverty, or plague, for the devil and *all* of his wicked agents are locked up forever and ever. Only righteous nations will be permitted to enter into what happens next, and that is the manifestation of the sons of God!

After the judgment of all the wicked, God will renovate the earth and heavens by fire: "looking for and hasting unto the coming of the day of God, wherein the heavens being on fire shall be dissolved, and the elements shall melt with fervent heat" (2 Peter 3:12). The elements refer to the present world system of evil, disease, germs, and the fallen nature and sinful residue that marked Satan's kingdom. When we see in 2 Peter 3:10 "in which the heavens shall pass away with a great noise," it does not mean there will be no more heavens. The Bible speaks of three types of heavens. First, there is the atmospheric heavens, which is the earth's sky and where the clouds are and the planes fly. Secondly, there is the starry space heavens, where the planet, suns, and universes exist. Lastly, there is the *planet heaven*, which is called the third heaven, and this is where God lives. When the Bible says the heavens shall pass away, it is referring to the earth's atmosphere and our fallen universe. They are the heavens that were corrupted by Satan and his army of fallen ones. The *planet heaven*, where God's throne is, has *never* been corrupted and, therefore, does *not* need to have Satan's pollutants burned from it. *Pass away* in the Greek is *parerchomai*, which means "to pass from one condition to another" and does *not* mean the earth or heavens will be destroyed. Ecclesiastes 1:4 says, "One generation passeth away, and another generation cometh; but the earth abideth forever." The earth and heavens will be restored back to their original states when God first made them, and there will be nothing left of the devil's corruptions. There will be no evil spirits, no fallen angels, not even a painting or a book. The only observance of Satan and his open rebellion against God will be the many openings in the renovated earth where mankind will be permitted to look down into the lake of fire and see the end of all who dared to rebel against God. The Amplified version of Isaiah 66:24 says, "Then they will go forth and look upon the dead bodies of the (Rebellious) men who have transgressed against Me; for their worm (maggot) will not die, and their fire will not go out; and they will be an abhorrence to all mankind." Let *all* creation *rejoice*, for the kingdom of God is come, and Satan is gone *forever*!

CHAPTER 14

The Manifestation of the Sons of God

Now that God has rid creation of all that corruption and restored the earth and universe to their original glory, He now moves His headquarter city the New Jerusalem from the planet heaven to the planet Earth. Revelation 21:2–3 tells us,

> And I John saw the holy city, New Jerusalem, coming down from God out of heaven, prepared as a bride adorned for her husband. And I heard a great voice out of heaven saying, Behold, the tabernacle of God is with men, and he will dwell with them, and they shall be his people, and God himself shall be with them, and be their God.

From earth, God will rule all creation; and from earth, God will establish the plan of populating the worlds. Notice that there are still inhabiters on the planet heaven even after God's holy city is moved to the earth. This fact reveals that all planets were truly made to be inhabited. Isn't it amazing that the God of *all* creation will rule from earth? The whole heavens has been changed to now accommodate the full manifestation of the glory of God. The full glory of God could *not* be released until *all* sin and corruption were done away with. Earth and the universe are now free to operate in the *full* blessing of God. They were once alienated because of the fall and out of unity with

God's obedient subjects on other worlds. It is when all of creation is unified with God that the full release of glory and blessing will fall. I call this the *all-in-all* glory of God. First Corinthians 15:28 says, "And when all things shall be subdued unto Him, then shall the son also Himself be subject unto Him that put all things under Him, that God may be ALL in ALL." The fullness of God and who He really is will be revealed to all creation. What glory, what goodness, what wonderful and amazing benevolence that will be released upon creation.

When we read Romans 8:19–22 (NLT), it is describing how earth is fallen and far removed from the all-in-all blessing of God. The manifestation of the sons of God is the time when earth and all of fallen creation is brought into this great blessing.

> For all creation is waiting eagerly for that future day when God will reveal who his children really are. Against its will, all creation was subjected to God's curse. But with eager hope, the creation looks forward to the day when it will join God's children in glorious freedom from death and decay. For we know that all creation has been groaning as in the pains of childbirth right up to the present time.

The whole creation understood what the fall of Adam produced, but now, Jesus—the perfect man—has ushered in the glorious liberty and unity of fallen creation back to God! Humankind being brought back into right standing with God directly correlates with the restoration of earth and all the planets that were once governed by fallen angels in their dispensation. Their liberty is attached with mankind because man was created to be their lights, the release of God's glory to their worlds, and the subjects that they are to govern. Now, the all-in-all glory will be manifested in all creation, and all will be inhabited and will together praise and magnify the mighty Elohim for His glorious plan in the heavens.

Earth is now the wonder of the universe. With the curse burned away, all of the gold, diamonds, amethyst, emeralds, and all other beautiful stones will be revealed in abundance, making the earth a stunning paradise fit for the arrival of the New Jerusalem from the *planet heaven*. The *planet heaven* has mountains made of brass. Zechariah 6:1 states, "And I turned, and lifted up mine eyes, and looked, and, behold, there came four chariots out from between two mountains; and the mountains were mountains of brass." It has streets of gold, transparent and clear as glass, and every beautiful stone known to man and some we don't know about. Surely, God would not move His grand headquarters city, the place where He rules everything in creation, to a lesser planet. What a magnificent city it is! It is 1,500 square miles with walls that are three hundred feet high. It is made out of pure gold like unto clear glass, and its gates are three hundred feet high and made of one giant pearl. There are twelve gates; each one has a transparent street of pure gold running through it. There are trees of life on either side of those streets that flow from the throne of God through the gates that will go out to the entire earth. All roads do *not* lead to Rome but rather to the New Jerusalem, where the eternal kingdom will be established forever. Can you imagine the mortal nations' reaction to viewing it as they approach it for the first time? They would see the walls and foundations made from jasper, sapphire, chalcedony, emerald, sardonyx, sardius, chrysolite, beryl, topaz, chrysoprasus, jacinth, amethyst, and many other precious material that are also located in the earth. I cannot describe the splendor and glory that will be witnessed by all as the light and glory of the mighty Elohim shine and reflect inside this incredible city. There will be no night there because God's glory will outshine the sun. In this majestic city are the mansions of the immortal sons and daughters of God and the rulers of the worlds. John 14:2–3 reminds us,

> In my Father's house are many mansions: if it were not so, I would have told you. I go to prepare a place for you. And if I go and prepare a place for you, I will come again, and receive you unto myself; that where I am, there ye may be also.

Millions upon millions of mansions for the many millions of kings and lords that live there. I know you thought that you would live in heaven forever, but that is *not* the plan of God. You probably believed that you would be a spirit on a spiritual plane somewhere in an invisible dimension—I know I did. Let me assure you that what God promised is real and tangible. He doesn't create the tangible, material worlds while He Himself exists in nothing or what I call invisibleness. No, beloved, He will be seen and worshipped publicly by the nations on earth and the ambassadors from the heavens. We will have immortal bodies and live in an immortal city, and as Revelation 21:24 says, "And the nations of them which are saved shall walk in the light of it: and the kings of the earth do bring their glory and honour into it." From here, the expansion of the kingdom will begin. How long the sons of God will live on earth, I am not sure, but God, no doubt, will begin to move quickly in the universe. The all-in-all blessing from God must begin.

CHAPTER 15

The Age of Ages and the Christian's Future

Now begins the most wonderful part of the Christian's life. Again, I must reiterate: that which exalts God and magnifies Him and His work is the correct revelation, and that which lessens or contradicts Him is incorrect. My sincere prayer is that the Holy Spirit will reveal the truth of all that the Lord Jesus has provided to His saints. Already, we have seen through God's Word how heaven is *not* our eternal rest, nor is it the place God will rule and reign from forever. What we are about to see in His holy Word now is so amazing and wonderful that our human reason and mortal mind cannot comprehend. The age of ages is the age of endless ages, one age after another forever. In this time without end, God will usher in the *dispensation of the redeemed*. This is where the innumerable people who have been redeemed and glorified as immortal beings will help God administer the affairs of the universe and rule and reign with Him. Consider Revelation 22:3–5.

> And there shall be no more curse: but the throne of God and of the Lamb shall be in it; and *his servants shall serve him*. And they shall see his face; and his name shall be in their foreheads. And there shall be no night there; and they need no

candle, neither light of the sun; for the Lord God giveth them light: and they shall *reign for ever and ever.*

Now, don't think for a minute that millions upon millions of immortal sons and daughters of God will only reign on earth. This certainly lessens God and is *not* in harmony with God's Word. God's kingdom is bigger and greater than anyone could ever comprehend. To limit His servants to earth *only* is not practical, logical, or scriptural. In the dispensation of angels, we saw how angels ruled the worlds on behalf of God, and it is a fact of Scripture that immortal man has been given dominion over all creation, *not* just the earth. In the Amplified version of Psalm 8:3–6, the Word declares,

> When I see and consider your heavens, the work of your fingers, the moon and the stars, which you have established, "What is man that you are mindful of him, and the Son of (earth born) man that you care for him? Yet you have made him a little lower than God, and you have crowned him with glory and honor. You made him to have dominion over the works of your hands: You have put all things under his feet."

The psalmist asked the question, "What is man, and why is he so important to God?" Nothing is higher than immortal man; he is only lower than the Elohim, and he has been crowned with glory.

Glory in the Hebrew is *kabod* and points to the splendor, honor, and state of blessedness bestowed upon one by God; and of course, *crowned* is a reference to kingship and authority. Kingship and authority over what? *Dominion* in the Hebrew is *mashal* and means "to rule, reign, and have authority over." Rule and reign over what? Man is given dominion over all the works of God's hands, and all things are under man's feet in relation to honor. All of creation is under the sons of God in authority and glory. When I say "all of creation," I'm including all of the other universes that make up the kingdom of God. Is there life on other worlds? The Word of God says emphatically, "Yes!" Look at Colossians 1:16–17 (NLT).

> For through him (Jesus) God created every-thing in the heavenly realms and on earth. He made the things we can see and the things we can't see—such as thrones, kingdoms, rulers and authorities in the unseen world. Everything was created through Him (Jesus) and for Him, He existed before anything else, and He holds all cre-ation together.

There are thrones, kingdoms, rulers, and authorities in the heavenly realms or universe. Visible, whether you can see them, or invisible things made of material substance, which is visible in its own realm. There are universes and planets that are so far away that they cannot be seen; they are invisible in that sense only, for they are the material work of the hand of God. The New Jerusalem is so far away, it is invisible to man, but when it is moved to earth, all will be able to see it. Remember, there are angels who didn't rebel in the dispensation of angels, and no doubt, they continue to serve God in their universes. They have been viewing the proceedings in our uni-verse and learning of the wonderful plan of God. Consider Ephesians 3:10–11 (Amplified).

> So now through the church the multifaceted wis-dom of God (in all its countless aspects) might now be made known (revealing the mystery) to the (angelic) rulers and authorities in the heav-enly places, this is in accordance with (the terms of) the eternal purpose which He carried out in Christ Jesus our Lord.

The Bible clearly states that God has established rulers in the heavenly realms, and it is also a published fact that immortal man has been given authority over them. The millions of planets in our fallen realm must be inhabited and guided by God's authorities. The angels lost this honor, but God made a special creation just like Himself— but a little lower—to replace them. Now the age of ages is come! Hear me, Christian, "If we suffer, we shall reign with him; if we deny Him He also will deny us" (2 Timothy 2:12). It is worth the persecution, the being ridiculed for believing in Jesus, for He is the King of kings and the Lord of lords, and He will reign forever and forever, and we will be kings and lords with Him reigning in the stars.

Jesus made everything that was made, and He shares it all with His saints. The church is called the body of Christ. Every member of the Lord Jesus will be given their share of the inheritance of Christ. We will have authority because Jesus shares it with us, "Oh, How I Love Jesus!" Jesus has dominion and power over everything. We read in Ephesians 1:20–23,

> Which He produced in Christ when He raised Him from the dead and seated him at His own right hand in the heavenly places far above all rule and authority and power and dominion (whether angelic or human) and (far above) every name that is named (above every title that can be conferred) not only in this age and world *but also in the one to come.* And He put all things (in every realm) in subjection under Christ's feet, and appointed Him as (supreme and authoritative) head over all things in the church which is His body, the fullness of Him who fills and complete all things in all (believers).

We will have dominion in the heavenly realms because we are the church, the Lord's body. He will fill the stars as He sees fit with the members of His body. The authority comes from the head (Jesus) and flows to the rest of His body (the sons of God). Romans 8:17 says, "And if children, then heirs, heirs of God and joint heirs with Christ; if so be that we suffer with Him, that we may be also glorified together." To be joint heirs with Jesus Christ is the highest honor one can receive. The glory and position and inheritance is mind-boggling. What wonders await the children of God.

Now when I say the sons of God or children of God, I'm referring to the immortal humans, those who have godlike bodies and attributes and who have received great glory and position in the kingdom. It is a fact of Scripture that the glorified children of God will reign as kings and priests forever. How could they be priests forever without worshippers to minister unto? How could they be kings forever without a kingdom and subjects to reign over? They certainly will not reign over one another or minister unto themselves. The answer is simple in the light of Scripture. They will minister and reign on other worlds. God has always had His creation rule planets for Him, and now His most prized creation is given that glorious honor.

CHAPTER 16

The Colonization of Planets

The last enemy that shall be
destroyed is death.

—1 Corinthians 15:26

Since death is done away with, natural nations will continue to populate the earth. The obvious question in view of the perpetual multiplying of the human race is, "How can earth hold so many coming generations?"

With the removal of the curse, childbearing is no longer a painful process but rather a pleasurable celebration of life. Women could have as many as one thousand offspring. Conditions will be perfect—perfect health, perfect life, and perfect love. The natural nations will live under the glory of the Elohim and flourish in every possible way. The plenishing of the worlds is an important aspect of the full glory of God. The purpose of the worlds' being populated is so that the nations can lift up their voices together on one accord and pronounce glory and praise to God with all other creation. There is a powerful release of God's glory upon His unified creation when they worship on one accord. God truly inhabits the praises of His people (Psalm 22:3) and will release His incredible benevolence upon them when they worship. We have a glimpse of this universal worship revealed in Job 38:4–7(NLT). God asked Job,

> Where were you when I laid the foundations of the earth? Tell me, if you know so much, who determined its dimensions and stretched out the surveying line? What supports its foundations, and who laid its cornerstone as the morning stars sang together and all the angels shouted for joy?

When God was creating earth, all the other planets and their inhabitants worshipped along with their angelic rulers. Notice they shouted for joy; they had joy released upon them uniformly as they praised God for expanding the kingdom—another world being created to give Him glory. "The heavens declare the glory of God; and the firmament sheweth His handiwork" (Psalm 19:1). This verse of Scripture tells us that God is ever expanding His vast kingdom and was delayed in this pursuit when the angels rebelled; but now, the expansion of His glorious kingdom is back on schedule. Christ came to restore man's dominion in the heavens (Psalm 8:3–6), and now that the planets have been restored to their original glorious condition as when God first created them, they are ready to be populated by immortal man and mortal man. God will populate these planets in our universe. They were populated before the fall of our universe led by Lucifer and will be again, and glorified man will be placed in an exalted position in the world to come. Hebrews 2:5–8 says,

> For unto the angels hath he not put in subjection the world to come, wherefore we speak. But one in a certain place testified, saying, "What is man that thou art mindful of him or the son of man, that tour visitest him? Thou madest him a little lower than the angels (Elohim); thou crownedst him with glory and honor, and didn't set him over the works of thy hands: Thou hast put all things in subjection under him, he left nothing

that is not put under him. But now we see not yet all things put under him."

The world to come not only includes being raptured up to heaven and living in a mansion in the New Jerusalem, but it also means the reestablishment of the kingdom of God over our fallen universe. The world to come will be the age where all creation will be in perfect harmony and synchronicity. All will be connected to God by and through the Holy Ghost to create the divine unity. All creation on all worlds will have God's rich blessings and a full release of the glory of God! Immortal man in particular will experience this glory because he will be the lights on these worlds. Just as Lucifer—the light bringer—and the angels that fell on their worlds were given authority and illuminated their planets by the light they received from God, so too, and in a greater way, immortal man, who was made a little lower than the Elohim (gods), will govern the worlds. Hebrews 2:5 indicates that not even the angels will have this kind of glory.

The word *crownedst* in the Greek translation is *stephano* and means "to reward for victory" and the glory and honor bestowed by God upon man in regards to his position in creation. The sons of God will be the lights upon all that they rule. Like the angels before them, God will manifest through them special wisdom and ability to rule well on their worlds so that all may share in the incredible, unsearchable riches of God. From the sanctuaries on these planets, all will assemble and worship the Almighty Father, Son, and Holy Spirit as well as receive governance from its king and lord. Yes, each planet will have its own king and lord, who will rule and reign on behalf of God; and just like governance on the new earth will be by God in person, immortal man will administer God's governance upon the human nations that will live there. All rule will come from headquarters—the New Jerusalem—and all will be connected by the Holy Spirit in some measure according to their status of glory.

Jesus said in Revelation 22:12, "Behold I come quickly; and my reward is with me, to give every man according as his work shall be." There will be different levels of glory and authority based on the believer's labor, but all governance will follow the pattern of the New

Jerusalem on earth. There will be nations and communities, and just as there will be no sin or death on earth, this same redemption will be carried out throughout all of God's kingdom. When Revelation 21:24 states, "And the nations of them which are saved shall walk in the light of it and the kings of the earth do bring their glory and honor into it," and Revelation 21:26, "And they shall bring the glory and honor of the nations into it," it is referring to *all* kings and *all* nations of every planet in all creation. Our God rules and reigns over all creation, and all will come to the holy city to honor the great God who is all in all. Our God is too big for our human minds to comprehend! All creation who are in right standing with Him in the kingdom recognizes that all things are created for Him and by Him and that He is so powerful—all things are held together by Him. One planet is not enough to exalt and honor Him; one universe alone cannot offer the praise due Him. All of creation must honor Him. There is a wonderful scene in heaven recorded in Revelation 4:8–11 of how God is to be honored by all creation.

> And the four beasts had each of them six wings about him; and they were full of eyes within; and they rest not day and night, saying Holy, Holy, Holy, Lord God Almighty, which was and is, and is to come. And when those beasts give glory and honor and thanks to him that sat on the throne who liveth forever and ever, the four and twenty elders fall down before him that sat on the throne, and worship him that liveth forever and ever, and cast their crowns before the throne, saying Thou art worthy, O Lord to receive glory and honor and power; for thou hast created all things, and for thy pleasure they are and were created.

God's kingdom is vast, and it was created to bring Him glory, honor, and praise. Dead planets and lifeless universes do not bring Him glory; however, worlds full of splendor and the unsearchable riches of Christ most certainly will!

God is the God of life and light—not void and darkness—and His glory will be everywhere in the heavens. The same nations that will be on the new earth will be in the worlds to come. Praise God! African, Asian, American, European, and all other saved nations will continue forever and ever. God is the perfect land conveyor. He knows exactly how many people can comfortably live on earth and on all planets, and because there will be no death, God will need to have the land he needs for his expanding kingdom. Life will rule in the heavens, and all creation will again praise and magnify the mighty Elohim from the sanctuaries on their worlds. All will be filled with the knowledge of the glory of the Lord, and "mankind"—God's prized creation—will multiply and spread throughout the kingdom. The world to come will be a social order of prosperity, life, love, and a close relationship with the God of all creation!

CHAPTER 17

The God Bodies of the Sons of God

(Luke 20:34–36)

O n these restored planets will be the sons of God who are immortal and the mortal children of God. All saved human beings are the children of God, but there is a great distinction between them in glory and power. There will be mortal rulers on the worlds, and because there is no more curse or sin, they will have great abilities similar to Adam before the fall. They will eat of the trees of life that God will place on their worlds and have perfect health. The leaves of the trees will produce perfect healing for all the nations. Remember, without sin, there can be no sickness or disease or anything that can corrupt or produce death. The verse in Revelation 22:2 is merely referring to the eternal health and life that will come from the leaves of these glorious trees. The mortal children of God will carry out the plan of God that was first given to Adam and Eve: "Be fruitful and multiply and replenish the earth, and subdue it." The nations of mortals will be spread throughout the stars, and they will be a great people. The Holy Spirit of God will be in them, and they will be connected to God through this rich measure of the Holy Ghost. I personally believe that whole worlds will be caught up in the Spirit and receive amazing messages from God Himself. Visions and trances and being spiritually translated with other brothers and sisters on other worlds will be a normal part of the social order. Consider Joel 2:28–29:

> And it shall come to pass afterward, that I will pour out my spirit upon all flesh, and your sons and daughters shall prophesy, your old men shall dream dreams, your young men shall see visions, and also upon the servants and upon the hand-maids in those days will I pour out my spirit.

All creation will be connected through God's Holy Spirit. Ezekiel saw the heavens opened and saw visions of God (Ezekiel 1:2); Daniel, in the Spirit, saw the mighty Elohim (Daniel 7:13–14); the apostle Peter saw heaven opened (Acts 10:11); Paul the apostle was caught up to the third heaven (2 Corinthians 12:1–4); and we see may saints of God who have had similar experiences in the spirit—so too will the natural nations have experiences. The immortal sons of God, however, will be different from their mortal brothers and sisters. Jesus says in Luke 20:34–36,

> The children of this world marry and are given in marriage but they which shall be accounted worthy *to obtain that world* and the resurrection from the dead, neither marry, nor are given in marriage, neither can they die any more; for they are *equal unto the angels* and are the *children of God*, being the children of the resurrection.

In the world to come, those who have participated in the resurrection of the Lord Jesus Christ will have a body like His resurrected body and become just like Him inwardly! These sons of God will be the conveyors and administrators to the worlds. This glory to be like God wasn't given to the angels or any other in all of creation. We will be rulers with the Lord Jesus Christ and have godlike wisdom, power, and ability. Only immortal man is given this type of glory and honor, for he alone is made in the Elohim's image and likeness—he (immortal man) is to be just like Him! Remember that 1 John 3:2 tells us, "Beloved now are we the sons of God, and it doth not yet appear what we shall be; but we know that when he shall appear, *we shall be like Him*; for we shall see him as he is." The immortal sons of God will be *just like Jesus*. What a tremendous honor to be just like God! It baffles the mind of creation the special glory and authority given unto the immortal man. Perhaps we can explain man's position by first seeing that God made man in His image and likeness, and he is the only one in creation that we know about that God made this way. Secondly, God Himself became a man so He could redeem us. God became a man! Creation bore witness that the Creator of all things became a seed and allowed Himself to be governed by the nine-month process of childbirth. He experienced the entire human condition so He could legally rescue humanity. "What is man that thou art mindful of him?" Indeed, whatever man is, God's will and grace upon him is the stuff of wonder in the heavens. If God would leave His God body and attributes to become one of them, what would be his plans and blessing for their future?

The God body and inner God makeup are certainly indicators of man's blessed future! As a matter of fact, Jesus calls the sons of God *light*. *Light* in the Greek is *phoster* and means "an illumination; a luminary or brilliant light." A luminary is a person who inspires and influences others in their area of expertise; but in an archaic sense, he is a natural light-giving body like the sun or moon. Both definitions describe the lights of the world immortal men are, for through the glory manifested upon and through their glorified God bodies, they will shine both in their inner being and in their body, much like Moses whose appearance was so luminous after spending time in the presence of God that the children of Israel could not look directly upon him.

> And it came to pass, when Moses came down from the mount, that Moses wist not that the skin of his face shone while he talked with him. And when Aaron and all the children of Israel saw Moses, behold the skin of his face shone,

and they were afraid to come nigh him. (Exodus 34:29–30)

Moses through continual contact with God became a great light. He received instruction from God how to govern the people, and he manifested great power and authority over Egypt. God even told him, "And the Lord said unto Moses, see, I have made thee a god to pharaoh, and Aaron thy brother shall be they prophet" (Exodus 7:1). What great miracles and power God wrought through the hand of Moses, who in type is a figure of the immortal sons of God, whose light will illuminate the universe. Just as Moses received God's law to govern the people, God's immortals will receive the laws of God and administer them in the heavens. And what about the legendary power that Moses yielded? The body of the sons of God will possess this same awesome power and ability. It will be capable of traveling billions of miles in a blink of an eye. It will be able to walk through material substances and many other incredible feats that we can only speculate about. When we see Jesus ascending to heaven in Acts 1:9–11, we notice that the disciples watched as He left the earth and flew in the sky, where the clouds received Him, and He left them. He could indeed fly and, being the real, authentic Superman, went to a place that no other could. No rocket or high-powered telescope can reach the third heaven, but Jesus, the only true superhero, rode a cloud to its lofty chambers, and the children of the resurrection will have the same body. Philippians 3:21 tells us, "Who shall change our vile body, that it may be fashioned like unto his *glorious body*, according to the working whereby he is able even to subdue all things unto himself." We will have the perfect body to enjoy the full blessing of God. Our taste buds, for example, will be able to enjoy the food God provides for us in a perfect way. In fact, all of our immortal bodily functions will be heightened to fully experience pleasure and joy to its maximum capacity. The body of God will feel as God feels, know as God knows. This alone is worthy of any suffering the believer may encounter at the hands of Satan. Can you imagine experiencing perfect God-love and perfect God-peace and perfect God-healing, and we can't comprehend the perfect God-power that God will give to the children of God! What I'm explaining is written in God's holy Word, and nothing can stop it from coming to pass. It is a fact that Christians will have this body!

Perhaps you are not a Christian. Maybe you are just a church-goer who has never been born again. Let me assure you that what you are reading is a fact. The unsearchable riches of Christ are so wonderful that it is hard for the natural mind to receive, but when you give your whole heart to Jesus, He will give you His spirit of wisdom and revelation in the knowledge of Him:

> The eyes of your understanding being enlightened, that ye may know what is the hope of his calling, and what the riches of the glory of his inheritance in the saints, and what is the exceeding greatness of his power to us-ward who believe, according to the working of his mighty power. (Ephesians 1:17–19)

God will open up your heart to see how wonderful Jesus truly is! And this is what awaits the true Christian. What glory, what joy, what wonder awaits the true born-again believers of Jesus Christ. This incredible inheritance is not for professors of Christ but rather possessors of Christ. It is not for those who love the world and blindly serve its fallen administrator. No, this beautiful glory is for those who "purify themselves, even as he is pure" (1 John 3:3), those who keep themselves "unspotted from the world" (James 1:27). The glory and honor of the born-again child of God will not be cheapened or devalued! We suffer persecution and ridicule. In fact, Christians are being killed in some countries, so don't think for a minute that the nonbeliever or one who does not pay the price of sanctification will receive this great reward. Oh, no, my friend.

> He that overcometh shall inherit all things: and I will be his God, and he shall be my son. But the fearful, and unbelieving, and the abominable and murderers, and whoremongers, and sorcerers

and idolaters, and all liars shall have their part in the lake which burneth with fire and brimstone, which is the second death. (Revelation 21:7–8)

That's right. Only those who suffer with Him will reign with Him; only those who overcome will inherit all things; this amazing body and the glory that goes along with it are for the faithful. His immortality is a scriptural guarantee. "As is the earthy, such are they also that are earthy; and as is the heavenly, such are they also that are heavenly. And as we have borne the image of the earthy, we shall also bear the image of the heavenly" (1 Corinthians 15:48–49). The Christian's future is mind-boggling!

CHAPTER 18

Ruling and Reigning with Christ

The Assignment Reward

Now, the children of God will be given their assignments in the kingdom according to their work here on earth.

> Every man's work shall be made manifest; for the day shall declare it, because it shall be revealed by fire; and the fire shall try every man's work of what sort it is. If any man's work abide which he hath built thereupon, *he shall receive a reward*. (1 Corinthians 3:13–14)

> Knowing that of the Lord *ye shall receive the reward of the inheritance*; for ye serve the Lord Christ. (Colossians 3:24)

The children of God will be rewarded with their share of the inheritance based on how they serve now. God is a just rewarder to all and will not grant the leadership of a world to one who does not labor to meet the criteria of such a reward. But all saints will rule and reign in accordance to their labor. Some will govern under a ruler of a world; some rulers will rank above other rulers. There will be a rank structure among the sons of God according to their service. The amount of glory one receives will determine the measure of their inheritance. An immortal could rule a province of planets and have authority over immortals who rule single planets. The inheritance of the kingdom will be given by God. They alone can make the judgment of who is deserving of what honor or glory. God has always had leadership and governance based on the glory bestowed upon one. Michael, the archangel, is one indicator in Scripture of rank within God's government. *Archaggelos* is the Greek word for archangel, and it literally means chief angel. In Ezekiel 37:24–25, we see how King David will rule Israel under the governance of God in the eternal kingdom on earth.

> And David my servant shall be king over them; and they all shall have one shepherd: they shall also walk in my judgments, and observe my statutes, and do them. And they shall dwell in the land that I have given unto Jacob my servant, wherein your fathers have dwelt and they shall dwell therein, even they, and their children, and their children's children *for ever*, and my servant *David shall be their prince for ever.*

The rule established by God on earth from the New Jerusalem will be the pattern for all governance everywhere.

If there are cities on earth, there will be cities where the sons of God reign. If there are human subjects under David who are under God, there will be human subjects under the rule of the sons of God who serve under God. There will always be thrones, dominions, principalities, and powers in God's kingdom just as there are right now. God is supreme, and all, in perfect unity, will follow His order and pattern. In Revelation 22:5, we read that God's children would reign forever and ever. The Greek word for reign is *basileuo* and means "to rule as king." Again, I ask the question, "Where will he rule as a king? And who will he rule over as king on a throne? What is the full inheritance of the children of God?" To fully understand the inheritance of the Christian, we must see what Christ Himself has inherited. In Hebrews 1:2, we read, "Hath in these last day spoken unto us by his son whom he hath appointed *heir of all things* by whom also he made the worlds." Jesus inherited all of creation and the worlds. Romans 8:17 declares, "And if children then *heirs; heirs of God* and *joint-heirs* with Christ; if so be that we suffer with him, that we may be also *glorified together*." Notice carefully that the children of God will be heirs of God and joint heirs with Jesus. The word "heir" means "a getting by apportionment" or "to be a sharer by lot." An example of how God distributes inheritances is seen in Numbers. Numbers is the fourth book of Moses in which the main theme is the organizing of God's theocracy upon His people Israel. God would speak to Moses, who would speak to the elders, who would communicate to those under them what the plan and wish of God are. His is the governing model for all in the kingdom. Those on thrones receive instruction and law from the Elohim, for by them do all things consist and are held together. In this way is governance theocratic. Numbers 26:52–56 says,

> And the Lord spake unto Moses saying, unto these the land shall be divided for an inheritance according to the number of names. To many thou shalt give the more inheritance, and to few thou shalt give the less inheritance; to every one shall his inheritance be given according to those that were numbered of him. Notwithstanding the land shall be divided by lot; according to the names of the tribes their fathers they shall inherit. According to the lot shall the possession thereof be divided between many and few.

Jesus and His coheirs have inherited the worlds and all will receive their portion by allotment. Think of that for a moment—we are sharers by lot of the worlds. We will possess and enjoy the worlds. You cannot inherit what you cannot possess, so the Word of Almighty God has declared that we are joint heirs with the Lord Jesus Christ in the heavens. "To an inheritance incorruptible, and undefiled, and that fadeth not away, reserved in heaven for you," declares 1 Peter 1:4. This inheritance has nothing to do with this present social system on earth but rather is incorruptible, undefiled, and is heavenly in its location, and it will be enjoyed forever. We know already that the headquarters city of God, the New Jerusalem, will be relocated to the earth from heaven. So we will not inherit the planet heaven, but from earth, God will begin to mete out the reward of the inheritance to His saints. God is bigger than our mortal mind can fathom. Remember, astronomers tell us that there is about forty sextillion stars, which are suns to other planets like our sun is to our solar system. How many planets to a star is unknown, but it is believed that ten percent of them are habitable. I believe Scripture is one hundred percent correct when Nehemiah 9:6 proclaims, "Thou even thou art Lord alone; thou hast made heaven, the heaven of heavens with all their host, the earth and all things that are therein, the seas, and all that is therein, and thou preserved them all; and the host of heaven worshippeth thee." The heavens consist of planets, and all their host worship God. In fact, sextillions of beings are no doubt worshiping the mighty Elohim. Let's consider Revelation 12:12a, where God speaks to the worlds who are still in unity with the kingdom. "Therefore rejoice, *ye heavens, and ye that dwell in them.*" Great multitudes dwell in the heavens—plural! Yes, my friend, the heavens are vast beyond our comprehension, and only our fallen universe is without inhabitants. "Is there any number to His vast celestial armies?" I don't think they can be numbered! Every child of God will receive his inheritance when Christ joins us with the other heavenly rulers to institute His rule over all creation. Ephesians 1:10–11 states,

> That in the dispensation of the fullness of times he
> might gather together in one all things in Christ,
> *both* which are *in heaven* and which are *on earth*;
> even in him; in whom also we have obtained an
> *inheritance*, being predestinated according to the

purpose of him who worketh all things after the counsel of his own will.

We will be one universal community—those in the heavens and those on the earth. Because God will live bodily on earth, earth will become the most important place in all creation. The children of God will begin their heavenly calling for God from His headquarters city, the New Jerusalem. "Wherefore, holy brethren, partakers of the heavenly calling, consider the apostle and high priest of our profession, Christ Jesus." Hebrews 3:1 tells us that all holy brethren are partakers of the heavenly calling. *Partakers* is *methchos* in the Greek and means "a partner." It is not only limited to earth because Christ is not limited to earth. His reign is over all creation: the earth, the heavenly realms—and we are partners with Him to spread the laws of God throughout the stars. Our calling is to rule and reign with Christ in the heavens. It is a heavenly calling, a partnering occupation with the great apostle to spread the glory of God into the heavens. Ephesians 2:6–7 says, "And hath raised us up together, and made us *sit together in heavenly places in Christ Jesus*; that in the ages to come he might shew the exceeding riches of his grace in his kindness toward us *through* Christ Jesus." *Sit* in Greek is *sugkathizo* and means "to give a seat in company with." It denotes a union with by association and the completeness that comes through that union. The children of God have been given a seat of authority in the heavens because of Jesus Christ, and in the age to come, we will be glorified together with Him. Jesus promises in Revelation 3:21–22, "To him that overcometh will I grant to sit with me in my throne, even as I also overcame, and am set down with my father in his throne, he that hath an ear, let him hear what the spirit saith unto the churches." The throne of God means the power and glory of God that stretches throughout all of creation. There will be no place where His authority is not felt, and He is going to call His servants to their assigned places of glory. All joint heirs with Christ will be glorified together with Him. They will receive his God body and share in the inheritance of the worlds. God's Word tells us that God "didst set him over the works of thy hands." Glorified man has been placed in authority over all creation;

whether thrones, dominions, principalities, or powers on other planets, they are all the works of His hands and, therefore, under the authority of the sons of God. "He put all in subjection under him, he left nothing that is not put under him," the Word declares!

I believe the entire universe will be available to the children of God, and wherever we go throughout creation, we will be recognized as the sons and daughters of God. Although we will receive great honor because of Jesus Christ's work of redemption, we will never be worshipped by creation. All praise and worship belongs to Christ and the Godhead. All will worship and magnify the mighty Elohim as before the fall. The immortal children of God will be the most thankful and appreciative for the unsearchable riches and glory that they inherit through Christ. We will indeed follow the example of the twenty-four elders in Revelation 4:10–11.

> The four and twenty elders fall down before him that sat on the throne, and worship him that liveth forever and ever, and cast their crowns before the throne saying, thou art worthy, O Lord, to receive glory and honor and power; for thou hast created all things, and for thy pleasure they are and were created.

Our thrones on other worlds—as represented by the crowns of kingship, which are only possible through Jesus—we will gladly cast our crowns at his feet. All will magnify the Savior forever! We will, with great joy, lead the inhabitants in the holy sanctuaries into unified praise of the glorified Christ and mighty Father and Holy Ghost. Yes, we will rule and reign with Christ. Yes, we are joint heirs with Him, but He alone is worthy of praise, and none in all creation will know it and appreciate it like the immortal children of God!

CHAPTER 19

The Grand Conventions

It is in the makeup of God to have days of commemoration. All throughout Scripture, we can see this particular part of His personality revealed. Consider Exodus 12:12–20.

> For I will pass through the land of Egypt this night, and will smite all the firstborn in the land of Egypt, both man and beast; and against all the gods of Egypt I will execute judgment: I am the Lord. And the blood shall be to you for a token upon the houses where ye are: and when I see the blood, I will pass over you, and the plague shall not be upon you to destroy you, when I smite the land of Egypt. *And this day* shall be unto you for a memorial; and ye shall keep it a feast to the Lord throughout your generations; ye shall *keep it a feast by an ordinance for ever.* Seven days shall ye eat unleavened bread; even the first day ye shall put away leaven out of your houses: for whosoever eateth leavened bread from the first day until the seventh day, that soul shall be cut off from Israel. And in the first day there shall be an holy convocation, and in the seventh day there shall be an holy convocation to you; no manner of work

shall be done in them, save that which every man
must eat, that only may be done of you.

God tells Israel how long the feast was to last and the requirements of it. The first and seventh days were to be holy convocations
for them. *Convocation* is *miqra* in Hebrew and means "a called-out
meeting" or "assembly of the public." God wanted Israel to assemble
and commemorate the awesome deliverance He wrought on their
behalf. As we can clearly see in verses 17 and 18, God gives them
the month and day. This yearly feast was to take place, and it will
be observed by the Israelite nations *forever*. All people of God will
celebrate this feast on their worlds with the nation of Israel. And why
is Israel so eternally honored? Let us never forget that this nation was
given the important task of protecting the seed of all humanity so
that the Messiah could legally come into the world. God needed a
people He could charge to perform this highly important task, and
the progeny of Abraham fit the bill. That being said, we must notice
that feasts and convocations will be a part of the social order in the
world to come. The celebration of the Godhead will be universal,
and the month and day for certain acts of God to be celebrated will
be determined by them. But I don't see any harm in using our Holy
Ghost imagination to try to figure out what some of the feasts might
be. How about the feast of the cross? Can't you just see the Holy
Ghost sharing with the universe the secret working of the cross and
the victory it provided for all humanity who accepted it? Oh the
joy of the worlds when the entire work of Calvary is known and
felt. There will be feasting and music and joy unspeakable. God will
honor us with His presence, and of course, when God's glory is in
a place, there is blessing and benevolence, prosperity and joy. These
eternal convocations will be glorious whatever feast we celebrate. The
singing and dancing and music will truly be heavenly, not to mention the food of the feast. Have you ever read the 150th Psalm?

> Praise ye the Lord. Praise God in his sanctuary:
> praise him in the firmament of his power. Praise
> him for his mighty acts: praise him according

to his excellent greatness. Praise him with the sound of the trumpet: praise him with the psaltery and harp. Praise him with the timbrel and dance: praise him with stringed instruments and organs Praise him upon the loud cymbals: praise him upon the high sounding cymbals. Let every thing that hath breath praise the Lord. Praise ye the Lord.

Every voice, musical instrument, and all of creation will praise God. I can almost see it now in my mind's eye: all the stars and everything on them in unity with all of the holy angels on their worlds on these holy convocations with one voice in worship. Holy, holy, holy Lord God Almighty! Can you hear it? It's bouncing through the galaxies from a thankful and grateful host of heaven. The mighty Elohim inhabiting the praises of His huge family and pouring His wonderful benevolence upon them all. There is no doubt about the fact that there will be eternal feasts and celebrations. Look at what Jesus says to His disciples in Matthew 26:26–30.

And as they were eating, Jesus took bread, and blessed it, and brake it, and gave it to the disciples, and said, Take, eat; this is my body. And he took the cup, and gave thanks, and gave it to them, saying, Drink ye all of it; For this is my blood of the new testament, which is shed for many for the remission of sins. But I say unto you, I will not drink henceforth of this fruit of the vine, until that day when I drink it new with you in my Father's kingdom. And when they had sung an hymn, they went out into the mount of Olives.

Jesus told his disciples that He would partake in the Lord's Supper in the kingdom of His Father with them. The eternal kingdom of God will indeed celebrate the Lord's Supper eternally. There will be no mortal or immortal human that will ever forget the body and blood sacrifice of the Lord Jesus. Yes, we will enjoy this great feast, and there will be pomp and grandeur like has never been seen before, when the "nations" (the redeemed people from the earth) will walk by its light, and the kings of the earth will bring into it their glory by day (for there will be no night there). Its gates will never be closed (in fear of evil), and they will bring the glory (splendor, majesty, and the honor) of the nations into it (Revelation 21:24–26). All nations will go to the holy city, the New Jerusalem, to present their gifts and offerings in majesty and great splendor. To view these great processions into the city to approach God would be worth any price of admission. All creation will do this—all creation everywhere! There will be great banquets of celebration on these feast days. Jesus told His disciples, "And I appoint unto you a kingdom, as my father hath appointed unto me; that ye may eat and drink at my table in my kingdom, and sit on thrones judging the twelve tribes of Israel" (Luke 22:29–30). Great feast of splendor and celebration with a great table of banquet with the Lord Jesus Christ awaits the sons and daughters of God.

CHAPTER 20

❦

The Wonders of the Universe

God's Expansion Continues!

Now the kingdom is established with no evil or anything to cause hurt or harm. All creation together is experiencing the all-in-all benevolence of God. Just when you think you couldn't see or receive any more wonder or glory, the mighty Elohim continues His awesome creative work. In addition to populating our renovated universe, He now moves into the outer recesses of dark space and begins to form new worlds and solar systems. Psalm 104:2 tells us that God "stretchest out the heavens like a curtain." It is the essence of who God is to create and expand. "The heaven of heavens cannot contain him." Everything and everyone must worship and praise Him, and when all existing creation has, then there needs to be more created to extol Him! Humanity will expand in the dateless future and so too will the creation of worlds. "The morning stars will sing together and the sons of God will shout for joy again." Can you imagine the awesome spectacle of seeing the creative power of God create? What joy and unspeakable, indescribable glory. But we will be there with them in the age of ages. New worlds and new explorations. Great light and great joy will flow through the galaxy as one sphere after another is created! We know that they will be round because all other planets are. And we know that they will be inhabited because everything follows the pattern of headquarters, and the planet earth is inhabited. As a matter of fact, all creation was in pattern to God's headquarters planet in the very beginning. The planet heaven is a sphere and is inhabited, and so too were all the worlds. Consider Job 22:14: "Thick clouds are a covering to him, that he seeth not; and he walked the *circuit* of heaven." God's first headquarters planet was a circle that He could walk around. Those who cite the volatility of the universe now must understand that meteors slamming into planets or black holes destroying stars is the working of the curse caused by the fall. The universe will be perfect at this time as the mighty Creator creates. "Jesus Christ the same yesterday, and to day and for ever" (Hebrews 13:8). We can see how He creates by looking at the planet heaven. The planet heaven is a rich round inhabited material planet that reveals the awesome glory of God. And so too will all planets! Jesus is perfect. There will be no darkness or planets crashing into other stars. All the heavens now will work in perfect synchronicity with the new stars He will create to manifest more glory and life in the kingdom. Everything will be perfect, and all will have no trouble performing their roles and occupations in the kingdom. All will have talents and abilities from the Lord Jesus and will be totally fulfilled in the realization of who they are created to be; whether a farmer or a manufacturer of goods, it will not matter. Everyone will be totally fulfilled and complete in who they are. It is a fact of Scripture that the mortal children of God will build and plant and have occupations. All will be prosperous, and there will be no poverty or debt. Take Isaiah 65:21–23:

> And they shall build houses, and inhabit them; and they shall plant vineyards, and eat the fruit of them. They shall not build, and another inhabit; they shall not plant, and another eat: for as the days of a tree are the days of my people, and mine elect shall long enjoy the work of their hands. They shall not labour in vain, nor bring forth for trouble; for they are the seed of the blessed of the Lord, and their offspring with them.

What a wonderful age. No poverty, famine, or plague. "Everyone will live in peace and prosperity, enjoying their own grapevines and fig trees for there will be nothing to fear. The Lord of heaven's Armies has made this promise" (Micah 4:4, NLT). But I also want you to understand the wonderful fellowship that will happen in the stars. Consider the spirit of the eternal subjects of the kingdom. "And on that day, says the Lord of heaven's Armies, each of you will invite your neighbor to sit with you peacefully under your own grapevine and fig tree" (Zechariah 3:10, NLT). Notice the beautiful, rich times of fellowship in the kingdom. I scoff at the space wars of the future where the aliens invade from outer space and swoop down on an unsuspecting humanity with lasers blasting, destroying cities and the planet. Not so, my friend. The Lord of heaven's armies is the Prince of Peace, and He has promised that there will be no more wars in the universe. This age is under the kingdom rule of the Lord Jesus Christ and the hospitality and sweet communion of the Holy Spirit. There will be visitors from other planets, but they will be fathers and uncles and cousins and friends you met at a uniplural fellowship of planets. Not only will the immortal travel the stars but also mortal children of God will be permitted to invite their friends and loved ones from other worlds to come and sit with them in their beautiful homes and enjoy their grapevines and fig trees. Great, great, great grandchildren will visit their great, great grandfathers on the other side of the universe! Surely, the God of family would not forbid the natural nations the pleasure of a good old-fashioned family reunion. What an amazing thing eternal life is. All of the progeny of humanity will never die, and they will marry and procreate and spread throughout the heavens. How will they travel to the other side of the universe? Will they step into transporter rooms like the one on the starship *Enterprise* and be beamed from world to world? God has technologies that are so far past anything we can fathom or imagine. Just reading the Bible; we can see many transportation technologies administered by God. In 2 Kings 2:11–12, we read of one of His methods.

> And it came to pass, as they still went on, and
> talked, that behold, there appeared a chariot of

fire, and horses of fire, and parted them both asunder; and Elijah went up by a *whirlwind into heaven*. And Elisha saw it, and he cried, my father, my father, the *chariot of Israel* and the horsemen thereof, and he saw him no more.

When God wanted to transport Elijah from the planet earth to the planet heaven, He sent a *chariot* of fire pulled by *horses* of fire and driven by *horsemen*. According to the scripture, they picked up Elijah and rode the whirlwind all the way to heaven. This is amazing technology, a flaming vehicle traveling on a whirlwind traveling at a speed so fast that the prophet Elijah arrives at his destination in a matter of minutes. And how about the mode of transportation used to transport Philip from the Ethiopian eunuch to the town of Azotus in Acts 8:39–40? We read,

And when they were come up out of the water, the Spirit of the Lord caught away Philip, that the eunuch saw him no more: and he went on his way rejoicing. But Philip was found at Azotus: and passing through he preached in all the cities, till he came to Caesarea.

This method of transportation is perhaps the most widely implemented by God, for we see it with the apostle Paul in 2 Corinthians 12:2, 4,

I know a man in Christ above fourteen years ago, (whether in the body, I cannot tell; or whether out of the body, I cannot tell, God knoweth), such an one *caught up* to the third heaven… How that he was *caught up* into paradise, and heard unspeakable words, which it is not lawful for a man to utter.

In these two cases, we see God transporting His servants through the method of the Holy Spirit. *Caught away* is translated from the Greek word *harpadzo*, which means "to take away by force." The force or power to seize one and take one from one place to the other is technique that boggles the mind. God used this mode of transport with Enoch in Genesis 5:24 and the apostle John in Revelation 21:10, and when we read in 1 Thessalonians 4:17, we see that this will be the way millions of Christians will be taken from earth to heaven. "Then we which are alive and remain shall be *caught up* together with them in the clouds, to meet the Lord in the air; and so shall we ever be with the Lord." In addition to these modes of transportation, one can only imagine the technological wonders that will be present in the kingdom as a result of God's perfect wisdom. In our fallen world today, we can see invention and technology that makes life better for the inhabitants of earth. Can you fathom the many technological wonders that will cover the worlds to make man's existence a blissful paradise? As I mentioned before, travel through space will be a normal part of the social order, and there will be some amazing forms of transportation. Yes, the mortal children of God will enjoy the amazing wisdom of God. *Wisdom* is *chokmah* in the Hebrew, where it refers to technical skills and special abilities to make something. God's inventions to bless man and open up the kingdom to all will be a staple of the kingdom. "And he will be the security and stability of your times, a treasure of salvation, wisdom and knowledge. The fear of the Lord is your treasure," Isaiah 33:6 tells us!

Mankind and all creation will enjoy the rich treasure of God's salvation, *wisdom*, and knowledge as His creative hand covers the heavens. The pattern of life will continue forever and ever as the mighty Father, Son, and Holy Ghost impose their will in the time-space continuum. These events we can extract from the holy Scriptures because it is the Father's will to reveal the blessedness that awaits the child of God. Psalm 25:14 says, "The secret of the Lord is with them that fear him; and he will shew them his covenant." *Secret* is *cathar* in Hebrew and means "to conceal or hide." But God's "secret is with the righteous" (Proverbs 3:32). He wants the church to know the wonders that await those that turn their backs on this wicked, worldly kingdom, and He wants this revelation of heirs of God and joint heirs with Christ to give His faithful subjects *hold-on power*! Hold-on power is the ability of the Holy Spirit upon the child of God to endure anything manufactured by the devil to remove them from the faith. Every wonderful revelation of the Christian's hope does this! This is why God reveals to His children what is hidden from the world. This amazing truth of God's Word will provide great encouragement to those who are saved and looking for that blessed hope, but to those that are lost and lovers of this world system, it will remain hidden. *Know this*: the love of the world cancels the revelation of the glorious kingdom from the heavens. The wonderful riches of Christ are communicated through His mighty Holy Spirit, not the spirit of this world. To receive the strength and vitality that God's truth provides, one must have it communicated to him by God's spirit.

When we read in Deuteronomy 29:29, "The secret things belong unto the Lord our God: but those things which are revealed belong unto us and to our children for ever, that we may do all the words of this law." It is indeed revealing that God has some knowledge reserved only for Him, and He alone will decide to reveal the secrets of the universe or not at His own discretion. One can only wonder about what God might do or create in the world to come, but that which is revealed through the Scripture belong to us. Can we see through the Scripture what God has done in the past? He is the same yesterday and today and forever, and He has revealed some things about Himself that we can know to help us understand what He will do in the future. Has He transported people in the past? Has He made worlds before, and how did He make them? All that is revealed in His Word belongs to the believer, and what is hidden is God's. To see the wonderful future of the Christian, we must look into His holy Word. The wonders of the world to come are hidden from the unbeliever but not the Christian. The hope of inheriting the kingdom is an essential part of our faith. Much like Abraham looked for a city which hath foundations, whose builder and maker is God (Hebrews 11:10), we look for the inheritance reserved for us on the worlds made by the Lord Jesus Christ. Notice that Abraham looked for a material city in the heavenly realm that was designed and made by God Himself. The New Jerusalem is a material city just like all other cities in the kingdom. Before Lucifer's rebellion, all the planets had cities. Remember the picture the prophet Jeremiah gave us of the social order of angels in the dispensation of angels: "And all the cities thereof were broken down at the presence of the Lord, and by his fierce anger." Jeremiah 4:26 tells us that cities and lands and houses are all material parts of the kingdom of God, and they will be enjoyed by His faithful children. The fellowship of the Holy Spirit, the riches and perfect healing coupled with the amazing inventions of the Elohim, will make this age the most wonderful to date. The expansion of the kingdom with all that exists within it will be great glory and wonder indeed! But without question, the beneficiaries who will enjoy the wonders of this age the most will be the immortal sons and daughters of God. With their position in the heavenly realms and their amazing, godlike attributes, travel through the kingdom will be exhilarating! The ability to fly from planet to planet or translate oneself in a second to the other side of the universe is an ability God gave the holy angels, but the children of the resurrection will have even greater power. *We shall be like Him.* God will give the immortal insights and abilities that no other creation will have. We will not be robots or automatons programmed to serve God either. No, not at all; but we will, through this wonderful state of immortal conversion, be so enlightened by the goodness and grace of God that it will be a great joy to willfully serve Him. Glory to God! What the fallen angels lost, we will gladly receive and in a much greater measure. I personally look forward to the Holy Ghost involvement upon my entire being to connect me to the Godhead in ways that the holy angels can only wonder about. We will be the lights of the worlds as God manifests His power and knowledge through us to bless all creation.

CHAPTER 21

How to Receive the Christian's Hope

You Must Be Born Again!

Redeemed man has a glorious future awaiting him! In the age of ages, we can only guess what other creation and worlds the great God will create. But the children of God will be there to witness it all. I know some will scoff at the revelations communicated in this book, but there will be those who honestly search the Scriptures with me to see if these words are "pie in the sky" or if they really hold scriptural integrity. I believe the great discerner of truth and magnifier of the Lord Jesus Christ has revealed to the open heart just how amazing salvation really is. While I understand that most of the Bible is about God's dealing with man and the earth, we cannot ignore the many scriptures that indicate to us that He is much, much bigger than man and earth alone. As a matter of fact, God raises glorified man to heavenly realms and realities. Also, we should remember that any revelation of Scripture that exalts, magnifies, and enlarges God and His work is correct revelation, and any revelation that limits and restricts God and His work is incorrect revelation. Our God is greater than our frail, fallen minds can comprehend, and we must always take the position of God's Word when evaluating His work. "O magnify the Lord with me, and let us exalt his name together," Psalm 34:2 states. In the light of His Word, we can see just how worthy God is of magnification. He is the Creator of all things, and everything He created, He created perfect and good. All of His creation who are still in unity with Him understand this, and they exalt Him; however, our fallen universe, of course, does not. The reason why the earth and its inhabitants do not with one voice magnify and exalt Him is because they are blinded from the truth by the god of this world. The glorious gospel of the Lord Jesus Christ is being systematically hidden from mankind. Yes, most of what is in this present evil world system is perpetuated and communicated by Satan. He has so concealed the truth about God that even some churches don't fully comprehend the full gospel and the true salvation of the Lord Jesus Christ. Some Christians can't explain what heaven is and what the requirement is to walk through those pearly gates, and something as important as being born again to receive this great salvation is hardly explained to the millions who go to church regularly. Just join the church, pay your tithes, and volunteer when there is a need in the church, and that will suffice. The blinding of humanity is at work in the land. The gospel message that Jesus first preached, "Repent for the kingdom from the heavens is at hand," is no longer the focus of most churches, and when they speak about the kingdom of God, they preach that it is in this present world now and not in the world to come. This error in doctrine has caused many a well-meaning believer to place his focus on the treasure of earth and this present evil social system. *Be a success in this world* and *bring the dominion of the kingdom to your circumstances* seem to be the new focus of the modern church. This blindness about the kingdom and what the Lord really accomplished is by design. Satan wants to steal the most glorious hope in all of creation—the hope of becoming the children of God! He has, through the past centuries, diluted and removed the glory of the gospel message. The message of immortality and the planet heaven, the ruling and reigning with Christ in the world to come, and being heirs and joint heirs in the inheritance of all things is hardly, if ever, explained in their fullness. The full gospel taught by the church will so inspire the Christian that nothing else will satisfy him, especially anything in this present evil world.

The hope of the Christian will separate him from the pollutants of Satan's kingdom. His desire will become eternal and not temporal. He will be consistently "looking for that blessed hope, and the glorious appearing of the great God and our savior Jesus Christ" (Titus 2:13). And he will say, like Paul in 2 Timothy 4:8, "Henceforth there is laid up for me a *crown of righteousness*, which the Lord, the righteous judge shall give me at that day, and not to me only, but unto all them also that love his appearing." His focus will be on the kingdom that is coming and not on this present evil social order. Many cannot see the brilliance of the kingdom because their main focus is on the world. I reiterate: the love of the world robs one of spiritual sight. The more one loves the world, the less he will desire the true things of God! I'm saying that one can be religious and still not understand the full truth of the kingdom of God.

> There was a man named Nicodemus, a Jewish religious leader who was a Pharisee, after dark one evening, he came to speak with Jesus. "Rabbi," he said, "we all know that God has sent you to teach us. Your miraculous signs are evidence that God is with you." Jesus replied, "I tell you the truth, unless you are born again, *you cannot see the kingdom of God.*" (John 3:1–3, NLT)

We see in this account in Scripture where Jesus tells the Jewish religious leader Nicodemus that in order to see the kingdom of God, he had to be born again. Nicodemus had spent a great deal of time in his pursuit of God. Training, education, and devout religious services was the way he attempted to have a relationship with Him. But now face to face with God, he is told that he has been using the wrong approach and that he can't *see* the kingdom of God. The word "see" here in this scripture is *eidon* in the Greek and means "to see, not so much the mere act of looking, but the actual perception of the kingdom and its realities." There are so many people with so many perspectives about God and how to have a relationship with Him, but when one is given the opportunity to hear directly from God on how to know Him and receive revelation about His kingdom, sadly, like Nicodemus, many don't understand. Jesus told him,

> You are a respected Jewish teacher, and yet you don't understand these things? I assure you, we tell you what we know and have seen, and yet you won't believe our testimony. But if you don't believe me when I tell you about earthly things, how can you possibly believe if I tell you about heavenly things? (John 3:10–12, NLT)

One's religion is not an indicator that he knows God, whether it is a formal religious approach or a nonformal religious approach. When I say formal religious approach, I mean a religious upbringing and affiliation to a particular religion or church. One might say, "I'm Baptist or Catholic" or any other religious identification, but that alone does not qualify one for the kingdom. Jesus says, "You must be born again." A nonformal religious approach is that which emanates from one's own mind, what an individual thinks and believes outside of a religion or church affiliation. Both perspectives come from a fallen mind that can only see through a darkened prism. *Know this*: to assume a way is right without comparing it to God's Word, which is always right, is a sure way to deceive one's own self. Jesus reveals to us why many can't receive and understand the kingdom. They are merely religious in their approach to God and cannot see. Only those who have the Holy Spirit can receive the revelation of the kingdom, so it is of utmost importance that one is born again.

Born again is *gennethe anothen* in the Greek and means "to be begotten from above." It literally means that there must be a transformation from God and a renewal in righteousness and true holiness to be saved. God gives all who believe the gospel of the Lord Jesus Christ the Holy Spirit. Consider Ephesians 1:13 (NLT): "And now you Gentiles have also heard the truth, the good news that God saves you. And when you believed in Christ, he identified you as his own *by giving you the Holy Spirit*, whom he promised long ago." To be born from above means to receive the Holy Spirit, who is from

CONCLUSION

To the born-again child of God, there are exceedingly great and precious promises given—eternal life and great authority and glory in the kingdom to come we know about, but there will be so much more. I like very much what we have extracted from Scripture into this book, but it doesn't even scratch the surface. The inheritance that awaits God's elect really is, as Paul described in Ephesians 3:8, "the unsearchable riches of Christ." I know that the glory and splendor of God and who He is can never be fully comprehended by His creation. He is past our finding out; even when we are immortal, we will only know what He reveals. Yet He does reveal to the saints what will encourage them and what will give them hope. "But God hath revealed them unto us by his Spirit," the Word of God tells us. Yes, God wants us to know about the Christian hope. It is the hope that gives us sustainability or what I call "hold-on power!" There is so much in this dark and evil world that is designed by the devil to steal the Christian's hope and weaken the Christian's strength. It is, therefore, very important for the child of God to be armed with the full hope that God reveals so that they may be fully armed against the devices of the adversary. Satan wants believers to not know what they are having faith in. He understands that the believer can only receive strength from what he knows to be a fact. In other words, he knows that if a Christian is foggy and unsure about heaven, then he cannot have a maximized faith about it. "What is heaven?" the devil asks. When one is doubtful about a thing, he cannot really have faith for it, and this is why Satan has attempted to keep the full hope hidden from the child of God. To believe heaven is a spiritual place, and you will be a spirit—a joyful spirit, but a spirit without a body nonetheless—is not only out of harmony with the Scriptures (which, by the way, are designed to give you maximum hope) but proves to the devil that you are unsure about your inheritance. If you are unsure, then your faith will be unsure—this Satan knows well. Our reward is not to sit around heaven all day, playing harps or floating on clouds. No, sir, my friend, God has something far greater than that for His heirs. What we have is a real and tangible inheritance waiting for us. "An inheritance incorruptible, and undefiled, and that fadeth not away, reserved in heaven for you," 1 Peter 1:4 tells us. We must learn to "look not at the things which are seen, but at the things which are not seen; for the things which are seen are *temporal*; but the things which are not seen are eternal" (1 Corinthians 4:18). When we begin to "set your affection on things above, not on things on earth" (Colossians 3:2), we will open our hearts to God's illumination and revelation. It is so amazing what Jesus has done for man. I encourage every Christian everywhere to hold fast to the blessed hope. Your future is so wonderful that I can't express in words the glory of it all. So let me close this revelation with the words of the apostle Paul in Romans 15:13: "Now the *God of hope* fill you with all joy and peace in believing, that ye may *abound in hope*, through the power of the Holy Ghost." Amen!

About the Author

Pastor Lee R. Bruner, the founder and pastor of Living Waters Ministries in Mesquite, Texas, is a native of Tulsa, Oklahoma. He has been happily married to Tracy Jones since 1990.

Pastor Bruner is a very charismatic and dynamic man of God. His love for God is evident as he takes on the role of shepherd with passion, commitment, and dedication. The recurring theme of Pastor Bruner's messages is that all believers should live under the direct influence of the Holy Spirit, who is responsible for the total work of salvation in the believer's life, empowering them to receive supernatural insight, wisdom, knowledge, and revelation in order to walk through every door God opens. Pastor Bruner preaches and teaches the Word of God with an emphasis on sound biblical doctrine. He ministers the Word with integrity, balance, and without compromise. He has a strong desire that all people go to heaven and consistently preaches messages designed to equip the believer to get involved in ministry and live in a way that honors God. This prolific preacher of the gospel has ministered all over the world, including in such countries as Holland, Germany, and Africa.

CPSIA information can be obtained
at www.ICGtesting.com
Printed in the USA
LVHW112020120520
655429LV00012B/200